Turning

Turning

A Year in the Water

Jessica J. Lee

HAMISH HAMILTON
an imprint of Penguin Canada, a division of Penguin Random House Canada Limited

Canada • USA • UK • Ireland • Australia • New Zealand • India • South Africa • China

Published in Hamish Hamilton paperback by Penguin Canada, 2017
Simultaneously published in Great Britain by Virago Press

www.penguinrandomhouse.ca

LIBRARY AND ARCHIVES CANADA CATALOGUING IN PUBLICATION

Lee, Jessica J., author
Turning / Jessica J. Lee.

ISBN 978-0-7352-3326-3 (softcover)
ISBN 978-0-7352-3327-0 (electronic)

1. Lee, Jessica J. 2. Canadians--Germany--Berlin--
Biography. 3. Swimmers--Germany--Berlin--Biography.
4. Swimmers--Canada--Biography. 5. Swimming--Psychological
aspects. I. Title.

GV838.L43A3 2017   797.2'1092   C2016-907177-4

Cover design by CS Richardson

Printed and bound in the United States of America

10 9 8 7 6 5 4 3 2 1

'Around us the illusion of infinite space or of no space, ourselves and the obscure shore which it seems we could touch, the water between an absence.'

Margaret Atwood, *Surfacing*

contents

the lakes

NORTH-EASTERN GERMANY

Baltic Sea

MECKLENBURG-WESTERN
POMERANIA

LOWER
SAXONY

SAXONY-ANHALT

BERLIN

POLAND

BRANDENBURG

SAXONY

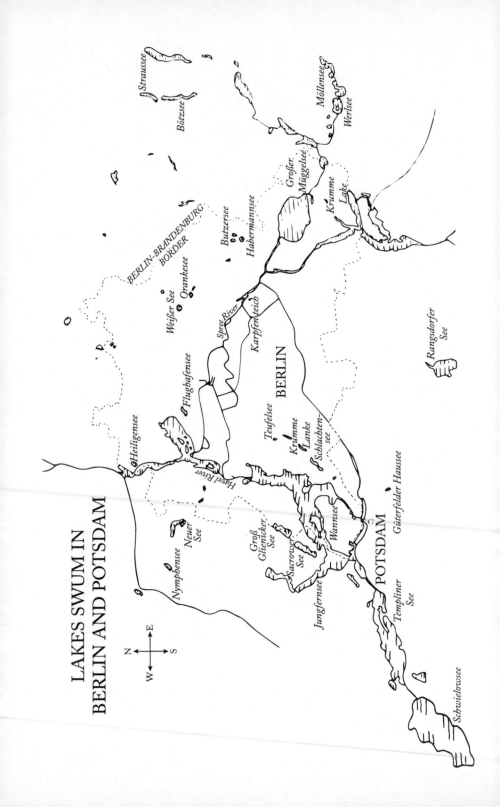

LAKES SWUM IN
BERLIN AND POTSDAM

N
W — E
S

Strausee

Börzsee

Möllensee

Werlsee

Großer
Müggelsee

Krumme
Lake

Butzersee

Habermannsee

BERLIN-BRANDENBURG
BORDER

Orankesee

Weißer See

Spree River

Karpfenteich

Rangsdorfer
See

BERLIN

Flughafensee

Teufelsee

Krumme
Lanke

Schlachten-
see

Heiligensee

Havel River

Güterfelder Haussee

Neuer
See

Nymphensee

Groß
Glienicker
See

Sacrower
See

Wannsee

POTSDAM

Jungfernsee

Templiner
See

Schwielowsee

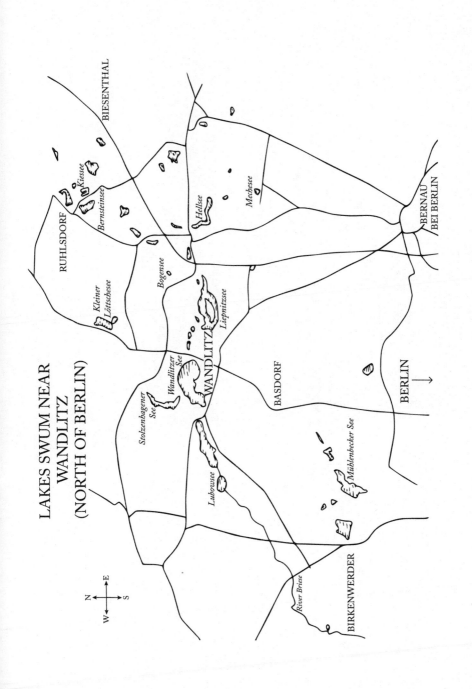

LAKES SWUM NEAR WANDLITZ (NORTH OF BERLIN)

BIESENTHAL

RUHLSDORF

Kiessee

Bernsteinsee

Kleiner Löttschesee

Bogensee

Hellsee

Mechsee

BERNAU BEI BERLIN

Liepnitzsee

WANDLITZ

Wandlitzer See

Stolzenhagener See

BASDORF

BERLIN →

Lubowsee

Mühlenbecker See

River Briese

BIRKENWERDER

N
W ←→ E
S

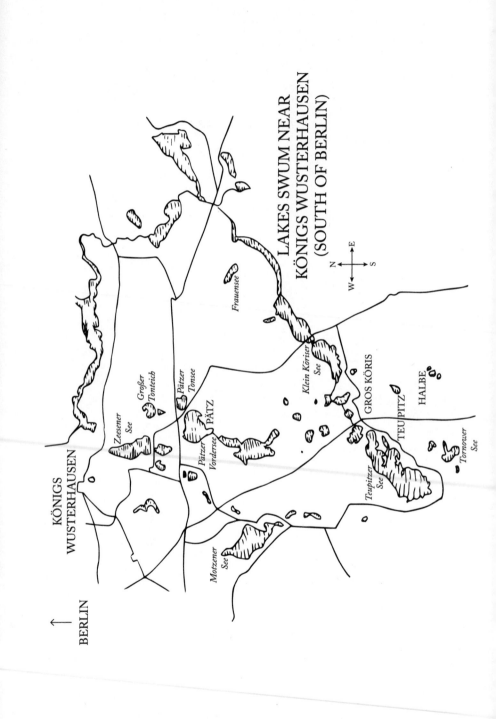

LAKES SWUM NEAR KÖNIGS WUSTERHAUSEN
(SOUTH OF BERLIN)

BERLIN

KÖNIGS WUSTERHAUSEN

Zeesener See

Großer Tonteich

Pätzer Tonsee

Pätzer Vordersee PÄTZ

Frauensee

Klein Köriser See

GROS KÖRIS

Teupitzer See

TEUPITZ

HALBE

Tornower See

Morzener See

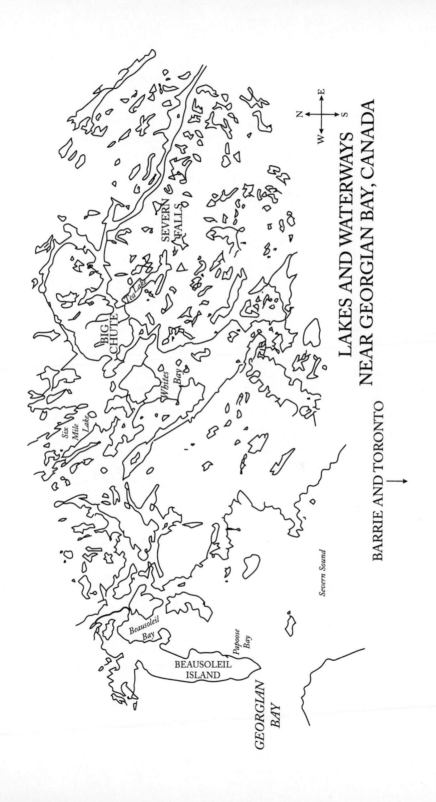

LAKES AND WATERWAYS
NEAR GEORGIAN BAY, CANADA

SEVERN FALLS

BIG CHUTE

Tea Lake

Whites Bay

Six Mile Lake

BARRIE AND TORONTO

Severn Sound

Beausoleil Bay

Papoose Bay

BEAUSOLEIL ISLAND

GEORGIAN BAY

prologue

It slips over me like cool silk. The intimacy of touch uninhibited, rising around my legs, over my waist, my breasts, up to my collarbone. When I throw back my head and relax, the lake runs into my ears. The sound of it is a muffled roar, the vibration of the body amplified by water, every sound felt as if in slow motion.

Above water, it is entirely light. The sun pours over the tips of the forest, washing the surface of the lake in warmth. I feel it on my face, warm in the air, as I lie afloat. Eyes open, there is only blue, no clouds. The edge of my vision is framed with pine, its golden pollen thick in the air.

Soon I will roll on to my front and submerge the rest of my body. I'll pull broad, arcing breast-strokes under-water, coming up between them for breaths. I'll feel the slight pressure on my palms as my arms sweep outwards, the gentle thrust of my legs as they spread and join again, the movement elliptical, repeated. Limbs stretched wide and then tight to my body again, my stroke as concise as a water strider dancing at the lake's surface.

But for a moment I stay on my back, moving at the border between air and water.

summer

Stratification: As the lake warms, the water separates into three layers. The coldest, the *hypolimnion*, sinks to the bottom. The warmest, the *epilimnion*, sits at the top of the lake. Between them is a zone of instability, the *thermocline*.

under water

A swimmer can sense the turning of the lake. There's a moment in the season when the water changes. It isn't something you can see, it's something you can feel. In spring, the winter ice melts, and the warm and cold of the lake intermingle, flowing together. In summer, as the lake grows warm, a green froth of algae caps the surface of the water, and when it cools again in autumn, the green disappears. The air thins. The leaves flash red and gold. And the water 'turns'.

You come to know the consistent cool of spring and the stagnant warmth at the top of a summer lake. When the water clears in the autumn, you can feel it: the lake feels cleaner on your arms, less like velvet and more like cut glass. And then winter comes, sharper than ever. Swimming year-round means greeting the lake's changes.

There is an English expression for the lake's changes: the 'breaking of the meres'. It describes the point in late summer when shallow lakes − meres − turn a turbid blue-green, algae breaking atop the surface like yeast froths on beer. The Germans also have a word for the green of summer: *umkippen*. It describes the point when the water has turned to slick green, fizzling with iridescent algae.

But the breaking of the meres and *umkippen* capture only that single moment of algal rupture, the death of the lake from too much algae and too little oxygen. We tend to notice the obvious thing – the emerging sheen of an algal bloom – and reduce a word's meaning to that tiny moment, that fleck of green on the surface.

The lake's turning – 'lake stratification' and 'overturn' – runs deeper, taking in an entire year's worth of changes in the water. Turning is perpetual. It points to the wider transformations in the water, as layers below billow and rearrange themselves beneath the surface. Even in winter, the lake is alive beneath the ice.

I long for the ice. The sharp cut of freezing water on my feet. The immeasurable black of the lake at its coldest. Swimming then means cold, and pain, and elation.

When I was twenty-eight, almost as if by accident, I was sent to Berlin on a five-month research placement. I moved into a second-floor *Altbau* flat, one of the crumbling, enormous apartments that looks straight out of a Stasi spy drama. And from this old place with an old cellar that had once been used for escape tunnels, I set out into a world of pine and silken water, of craggy cobbles and peeling paint.

Berlin resembled the other places I've called home – Canada, Britain – but only in glimpses: in the way the skeletal pines would edge the lake, in how the old stones would grow thick with moss. Pain, brightness, loss and renewal were layered in the landscape: in the lush shade of Tiergarten, which in my grandfather's days was barren, razed and desperately carved up for allotments, and in the crooked edges of concrete that had slowly been dismantled as kids my age grew up. I was three when the Berlin Wall came down. I don't remember it, but I came to know it in my own way.

The footprint of the Wall was turned into a hiking trail. Pavements stopped you in your tracks, *Stolpersteine*, brass stumbling stones marking the lost. Roads radiated out like a dial, a stretched palm pressed on to the city. I thought the roads here had to be so wide, if only to hold the ghosts.

Half a year later, as I was retreating from the deep end of depression, I surfaced with the bizarre notion that the solution to my problems lay in swimming. I felt furious that I had succumbed to the dark vacancy of my moods, as though it were my fault. My heart was broken. Above all, I thought that swimming might help me find some new place in the world in a year in which I'd changed address five times. A place in a city that wasn't mine, and that held layered in its streets a century of change and grief, ghosts in the landscape. Naively, perhaps, I believed that if I could find that place in the middle of the lake where every feeling slipped away, I might undo the hurt.

I'd moved again – this time into a stark white room with ceilings thrice my height – but spent only a few moments unpacking and settling in before turning my eyes to the map. The city at its centre, cut through by a fan of broad avenues and the rivers, the sudden countryside at its edges. Hundreds of spots of blue multiplied exponentially as the city lines crept into the surrounding land. These lakes and rivers – their intricate weave of water laid on to the flat North German Plain by retreating glaciers in the last ice age – had worked a tiny hook into my heart, and I could do nothing for it but swim.

Perhaps it was a drastic response. In depression, I had become someone I hadn't wanted to be, emptied and hardened. I felt that I had to respond to it in kind, as if lake water might blast away my sadness and fear. So I decided to swim for a year, in the hope of finding some reserve of joy and courage in myself. It was a means of greeting the ghosts – mine and others – as they appeared around unknown corners. I knew there was no untouched landscape here: there is hurt that cannot be undone. I wanted to find a way to negotiate it, to live with it.

Of all the lakes near to the city, I planned to swim in fifty-two, a whole year's worth, stretching my swims out through each season. Prone to rules, I kept the parameters simple: no cars, no wetsuits. I could take friends from time to time. My daily life would continue as normal. I was in the final year of my doctorate, finalising and refining a dissertation in environmental history. I was living an ocean away from family and home. There was pressure to hold things together. Swimming would be a way of staying with my fears, a way of staying in place. Above all, I sought to find some balance in it.

The summer in Berlin began coolly and then arrived fully formed, hot. Bright swathes of sunlight stretched over the cobbles, and the sky painted itself cornflower blue. The temperature rose and the air thickened only slightly as a hot, dry June settled on the city.

I looked at the map, traced my fingers over the lakes I knew – Krumme Lanke, Weißer See, Liepnitzsee, Bötzsee, Mühlenbecker See – and decided, as if by habit, to start at the beginning. Krumme Lanke, my first German lake.

the swimmer's view

There is a bay in central Ontario, two hours north of Toronto, in the heart of Canada's 'Cottage Country'. It is a place of rock, water and vast expanse. I swim there whenever I'm back in Canada, but for most of my childhood I wouldn't swim in it at all. The depth and the darkness of the water kept me on the shore, terrified. The tangle of water milfoil in the shallows, to my mind, was a danger: grasping hands of water weed, clutching at my legs. It wasn't a place for swimming.

But it was the land my parents chose. Both immigrants to Canada, they set about approximating the ideal life. My father arrived in the early 1970s, carrying twenty dollars in his pocket. He'd left school in Wales at sixteen, set off across Europe doing odd jobs until he boarded his first Boeing 747. He arrived to a tangle of Canadian suburban houses in need of renovation, so he became a travelling salesman, replacing ageing clapboard and glass up and down the province. Within a decade, he was running his own business, hiring other salesmen like him.

My mother arrived at twenty in 1974, speaking English only in fragments. Her credits from secretarial college in Taiwan weren't recognised in Canada, so she was sent to complete grade twelve at her local high school. She spent the year out of place, longing for home. And then she married my father, an anchor in a foreign land.

By the 1980s, our family was living in the Canadian suburbs, learning to be Canadian. My sister Nika and I were enrolled in primary school on weekdays, Chinese school on weekends, ice-skating lessons, summer camp, ballet. We moved from one suburb to a nicer one. My father designed the logo for his home renovations business, a maple leaf to dot the 'i'. We were sent for swimming lessons at the YMCA, because swimming lessons seemed essential in a land full of water. Neither of my parents could swim.

Like my mother, we spoke Mandarin at first, but in time the words disappeared. We spoke only English at home. In school, they taught us French.

Now, halfway across the world, as I've learned to speak German, I think of this. Of the language I lost and those I've gained. Of the places that have reshaped who I am and where I find home.

I remember the sound of my mother walking through the door at the end of the day. '我回來了', '*Wǒ huíláile*' — one of the refrains in Mandarin that she repeated, as if speaking to no one. I've always thought this meant 'I'm home', but I've learned that it means only, 'I'm back', or 'I've returned'. But '回', 'return', the small box tucked safely within another box, is a kind of comfort. The origin of the character is in a spiral, referring to a kind of regularity, the rotation of coming and going. Home as the place you return to.

From time to time, the words take shape in my mouth when I walk through my apartment door in Berlin. A kind of routine, the same way the patch of shore-line from which I swim represents safety. Fragments of Chinese slipping out between English and German, as I press new words and places into place. Return. Home is as much in a language as it is in a landscape.

The German word *Landschaft* implies a cultural landscape. It's built into the very idea. To speak about landscape in Germany is to speak of a place shaped by people, and given the past century's history, it hasn't always been easy to speak about. But agricultural fields, the romanticised places of forest and hillside, the many-storied rivers that traverse the country: all of these are cultural, on some level, shaped by and shaping culture.

The name Berlin, so the story goes, stems from an old Slavic word for 'swamp'. Hardly an attractive beginning, but it is an accurate name nonetheless: Berlin is built on wet ground. The Spree and Havel Rivers slide across the city, damp cobbles edge the canals, ground-water rises from the sandy soil. A ring of water surrounds Berlin: a speckled landscape of lakes. Fresh water rushes into former sand quarries, moorland slopes into marshland, rivers slip and swell across the flat ground.

Brandenburg surrounds Berlin. A countryside at odds with the city, it is the place I least expected to love.

Berliners joke about Brandenburg: 'its poverty', 'its backwardness', 'its bigotry'. They ask if I've been given a hard time by neo-Nazis. They warn me that I'll have to improve my German skills if I'm to make it. All of this holds a grain of truth.

But before any of that, I knew it for its water. To leave the city, to swim, you need to know Brandenburg. It's a place of summer afternoons, holiday homes and forest trails. It's a place where silviculture thrives, where people farm and people live. It's a place that's made me stronger.

Picture an eagle with its wings outstretched. That's Brandenburg. Berlin is at its heart. To know Berlin's landscape means to know Brandenburg's too.

In 1862, Theodor Fontane, one of Germany's most celebrated nineteenth-century realist writers, began to document his travels through the region. His five-volume *Rambles Through the March of Brandenburg* took twenty-seven years to complete and remains one of the most popular works of German travel writing. While the book has remained popular in Brandenburg, the relative inaccessibility of the landscape until 1989 has meant that the book has been somewhat overlooked amongst English-speakers. It remains, however, a detailed and personal portrait of Brandenburg before the turn of the twentieth century, mindful of its precariousness in the face of industrialisation. From the forested, sparsely populated north-west of the region to the marshland at its east, his accounts speak of a place grounded in water, a place that came to thrive through its aquatic prosperity.

I began reading Fontane's *Rambles* when I moved to

Berlin, translating passages from German in fragments, searching the text for lakes and towns I knew. His was a landscape shaped by storytelling and by memory. His was a Brandenburg untouched by the twentieth century, layers beneath the place I've come to know.

Like me, Fontane spent his early career in London, documenting his life in the city, and his travels in England and Scotland. The British are known for a love of landscape writing, an intimate love of historical minutiae written in the ground. Fontane brought that love to Brandenburg, attempting to discover his home landscape lest some foreigner do it on his behalf. A hundred and fifty years later, I can't ignore the humour in this.

The borders of Brandenburg then were somewhat different, and the fields are now more monotonous. In the centuries preceding and succeeding Fontane's *Rambles*, it changed dramatically, but many of the places Fontane documented remain. The lakes, most of all.

The North German Plain, formed during the last ice age, is a lowland shaped by water: the cratered lakes carved into the ground, the north-flowing rivers formed from glacial spillways and the porous sheath of sand left behind by the ice. Many of the dips and depressions that make up the three thousand or so lakes in Brandenburg arrived as the glaciers retreated across the north of Europe some ten thousand years ago. It's a place marked by flatness, by flat agricultural ground crowned with forest. Today, its highest points are wind turbines, scattered like seeds across the land.

In many places, the region turned to marsh. In the Havelland, west of Berlin, Fontane wrote that cattle would get stuck in the mire while searching for dry ground. East of the city, the Oderbruch was so waterlogged it stood under ten feet of water in the spring. Mists hung over the marshes, impenetrable wastes vastly unlike the fertile Fens of England. The marshes of Brandenburg kept people out. That was before the land was drained and dried out in the seventeenth and eighteenth centuries under Frederick William I and his son, Frederick the Great, with the help of Dutch engineers. Over the course of a hundred years, what was malarial marshland became monotonous, productive field. Along with the marshes, Brandenburg lost much of its native flora and fauna.

There aren't bears here now, but there are wolves. Small numbers of them, coming back from the east, travelling amidst the trees. Hunted to extinction over a century ago, protection has brought them back to Brandenburg's endless stretches of forest. A third of Brandenburg is woodland, but mostly the predictable, managed kind: Scots pine in succession, awaiting harvest.

In the flat, deeply-altered spaces of Brandenburg – cultivated forest, canalised marshland, restored moorland – there is no landscape without people. There is no wilderness.

Instead, there is intimacy. The intimacy of a landscape shaped by history, of a place that holds the record of human joy and sadness. It is a place that is more than simply human: of mushrooms, the element of surprise; of mosses, their complexity just out of reach. Above all, it is a place of water. The most intimate of all.

Rilke, in '*Die Gazelle*', describes the moment in swimming when one finds oneself reflected in the water:

wie wenn beim Baden
im Wald die Badende sich unterbricht:
den Waldsee im gewendeten Gesicht.

(as when,
while swimming in some isolated place,
a girl hears leaves rustle, and turns to look:
the forest pool reflected in her face.)

In the stillness of the lakes, the border between nature and culture is thinned. Swimming takes place at this border, as if constantly searching for home. Water is a place in which I don't belong, but where I find myself nonetheless. Out of my culture, out of my depth.

Swimming out of my depth still feels new and terrifying. Between strokes, a gap opens and is filled by every horrible thought of what could happen, every idea of what is beneath me and an overwhelming darkness. Thick and liquid fear rises in my chest. And I panic.

I now know how to work with this. Lashing my eyes to a spot on the horizon, I swim forward and think only of what is above the water, that snow-globe arc of a world full of beauty. The 'frog's eye view', says Roger Deakin. I stay there, and feel only the sensation of water running across bare skin. Fear can be dissolved.

But once in a while it returns, a heavy pressure that weighs like deep water on my heart. And I'm at the bottom of the YMCA pool, looking up through the clouded, chlorinated blue at the feet of other children. Their legs are dangling off the edge of an enormous yellow foam duck. I can't breathe. I'm underwater. I don't know what to do, and I don't know how to swim.

It's one of my oldest memories – I don't now know how many of its scenes have been added by my parents' recollections, but I know they've tampered with it. Otherwise I wouldn't see them so clearly, banging their fists on the observation deck window, trying to get a lifeguard's attention. It's the same every time. They look down on the pool and bang their fists, and their love and fear is liquid clear. I'm at the bottom of the pool staring at dangling, tiny feet. The distance feels immeasurable.

The YMCA in London, Ontario had one of those retractable-bottomed pools, which could go from shallow paddling pool to diving pool with the press of an enormous red button. We used to watch the floor heave upwards before swimming lessons and downwards when the big kids would arrive. So it could have been really deep. I was only three, maybe four years old; the water felt twenty feet deep.

I sit on the bottom for an eternity, water weighing on me, before a whistle blows and a lifeguard in red shorts breaks the surface and swims down, grabbing me in one arm and drawing me to the surface as if it's the easiest thing in the world. The distance from the bottom of the pool to the world above is nothing to an adult.

They didn't give me CPR, but for a time I wished they had. As if it would justify my later terror, render it serious. I remember the fear and the anger. My parents' anger. It took far too long for someone to notice that I'd fallen off the yellow foam duck. Someone, I would insist for years, had pushed me. Why had no one noticed?

Now, I laugh a little at the idea of drowning because I'd fallen off a floating foam duck. Nothing about it makes the fear any smaller, any less real, when I'm in the middle of a lake and it comes back, and I panic all over again. But the sight of an enormous foam animal at a kiddie pool or at the beach will still send me into inexplicable laughter.

We're laughing loudly, and the leaves are shaking in unison. The wood was still before we got here, but now the little slips of green leaf are in movement with the wind, and light flows in between them and falls to the muddy ground. I turn back and look at Sennah, Rosie and Joy, asking where they would like to stop. They're over from Canada and I'm trying my best to show them the city. The best spot, I tell them, is around the corner.

They trust me, so they walk on, still laughing about some joke while I move ahead into the silent wood. Just a few yards ahead, I'm able to greet the silence, to have a moment's breath. But I'm glad for their laughter, the raucous noise and the company. It is only the beginning of June, the beginning of my year of swimming, but I'm already afraid I'm going to be alone in this.

The lake is to our left, and as we round the curve of a small inlet it shines blue and black under the sun and wind. In the shelter of the wood it felt warmer, but here on the small, terraced arc of sand, the wind skips out across the surface, and it feels less like summer. My friends look wary.

Undressing, I step into the water – familiar, but I haven't been here since New Year's Day, when it was capped with ice. Now that it's warm again, I think not of the ice but of the sun-drenched summer afternoons I spent here last year, when I first came to Berlin. I swam in Krumme Lanke often when I moved to the city, before I knew any other lake here, when I hadn't yet made any friends. I'd moved and taken a research position in the city's suburbs, working away at my dissertation in environmental history. I'd begun cutting my work days short by cycling to Krumme Lanke, its thin strip of lake water marking a crisp edge along the Grunewald.

The Grunewald sits on the west side of Berlin, a thick swathe of green forest – literally, *grüner Wald* – preserved from development. Once a royal hunting reserve, the forest here served as the only accessible analogue for countryside for West Berliners during the Cold War. It was my first experience of a forest in Berlin. Krumme Lanke, one of its many lakes, means 'crooked lake'. The name stems from Slavic – as so many of the names in the east of Germany do – for 'river bend', 'crook', 'meadow' and 'bay'. It is a long, skinny lake, curving at the eastern edge of the forest.

Those early days in the city, I swam alone and often, leaning my green bicycle against waterside trees and undressing between the leaves. Most days, a nearby pair of old women would swim naked and dress in the bushes, and some athletic swimmer would trace lines up and down the lake's length. I was less ambitious. Swimming a steady breast-stroke to the lake's centre, I would turn on to my back and spread my arms wide, blue sky stretching tree-top to tree-top, an entire world spinning with me at its centre. I didn't know any people in the city, but I found in the middle of the lake a small, self-centred security, like a pin stuck into a map.

Now, I'm swimming out into the centre again and the water is cold – it's only just June – and my friends are standing up to their ankles at the shore, shaking their heads. Midway across, I tread water and look down the lake's length, grass-lined and whipped into small crests of wave. I'm cold and realise I'm in the shadow cast by an enormous cloud, so swim out farther to a blue and sun-drenched swathe of water, calling for my friends to do the same. Sennah and Joy have made it up to their waists by now, shrieking, and still eyeing me suspiciously. Rosie watches from the shore. Perhaps I ought to swim back.

When I reach them, Joy reminds me that she can't swim, and for a moment I'm mortified. I had lost myself so quickly. I know her fear well. But she assures me that she is having fun, isn't going out of her depth. She can't quite believe that in a city this size it's so easy to find such a quiet lake. The belief that enough time spent in Berlin lakes will convert anybody to open water swimming isn't new to me, but I am relieved to hear it from her so quickly. She gets it. I paddle nearby, where the shallows drop off, and watch as she and Sennah bend their knees and submerge their shoulders in the cold.

A swimmer knows a lake through sensation; through moving from the shore-line to the centre, through the feeling of the water. Warm, thick. Cold, sharp.

But sensation alone won't explain a lake to me. It won't tell me how the lake came to be in the landscape, or how its seasonal changes take place. It won't make me less afraid. For this, I turn to books. Early in the summer, I take out all the books on limnology from the Staatsbibliothek, old classics and new textbooks, as if I could encircle my fear with knowledge.

As a science of lakes – or, more accurately, a set of sciences related to inland waters – limnology has been intimately linked to Germany. The earliest institute for freshwater research – the Hydrobiologische Anstalt in Plön, on Germany's northern coast, now the Max-Planck-Institut für Limnologie – was founded in 1892, and one of the key scientific journals of the field, *Internationale Revue der gesamten Hydrobiologie und Hydrographie*, was established in 1908. The field itself was named by a Swiss scientist, François-Alphonse Forel, whose turn-of-the-century study of Lake Léman in Geneva introduced the term with the intention of creating a unified, broad science, encompassing all matters of lake study. The biological, the physical and the chemical.

It is a field that thrives in a few pockets of the world, especially those plentiful with fresh water. The Great Lakes, near where I grew up, are a central focus. The Lake District in England has attracted study. And unsurprisingly, the region of Berlin and Brandenburg – with its wealth of lakes and rivers – remains a crucial focus for German limnologists.

I'm not trained as a scientist, but an environmental historian must be adaptable. For this reason, I jump between history, ethnograph and botany. Archives, interviews and plant keys. As a swimmer, limnology is another kind of key. A way to read the lakes.

A lake is shaped by all that it contains. At its most basic, it is a water-filled basin surrounded on all sides by land. But each lake takes its character from the ground surrounding it, the water that feeds it and the biotic forms that inhabit it.

I start with a somewhat outdated classic of the field: *A Treatise on Limnology* by G. E. Hutchinson. His texts span lake biology and limnological botany, but the foundation of limnological study is in the geology, physics and chemistry that shape the lake in the first place.

Hutchinson begins with the formation of lakes. Were they left by glacial retreat, by volcanic activity, by tectonic movement? The non-anthropogenic lakes in Berlin and Brandenburg were shaped by glaciers, through meltwater flowing in tunnels beneath the ice and kettles left behind as the ice sheet receded. Ice accounts for not just the shape of the lakes, but for their sandy, clayey or silty lake-beds.

All of this matters to me, whether I realise it or not. The shape, depth and ground of the lake will help determine when the ice comes in winter, how completely the lake will freeze. So I find myself checking data online: lake depths, historic ice cover, water quality. The seasonal changes in a lake will be determined not just by shape, size and clarity, but also by wind skipping across the water's surface, a subtle turbulence that mixes the water. The clarity of the water matters too, in whether it allows sunlight to the lake floor or whether the lake is at risk of stagnating in the summer. Levels of plankton and bacteria will affect the water's clarity, and, in the interconnected world of a lake, they'll move deeper and shallower according to the light. If nutrient levels rise too high, and oxygen levels sink too low, 'eutrophication' – lake death – can occur.

I mark out pages in Hutchinson's *Treatise*, pressing pink Post-It notes into its ageing leaves. Like I'm learning a new language. I compare his text with newer textbooks and write emails to local lake scientists. I'll watch for the differences between each lake as I swim. I want to feel it in the water.

a short spell

The sun is at its hottest, and there isn't a cloud to be seen. We're rounding a green corner and there's a railway bridge ahead, beyond which I can see a small copse of trees. We need to be there, nearer to the water's edge. The heat bears down on my shoulders.

As if by magic – which I know can't last – a group of friends have decided to join me at Templiner See. Fifty-two lakes is a lot, so I'm grateful for the company. I'm only a few days into my year of swimming, and already it feels I've taken on too much.

They're trusting me to navigate, though I've never been here before, and they've absent-mindedly followed me for a mile to get here. I worry their patience is growing thin. They must hate me. It's too hot to be out here, looking across the enormous expanse of deep blue. I pray silently that the right spot will materialise around the next corner. It has to.

Potsdam orbits at Berlin's edge like a small satellite planet. The capital of Brandenburg, it sits quietly outside of Berlin, an ordered scene of palaces and gardens cut through with busy roadways. Last winter, construction workers found an unexploded Second World War bomb underground in the midst of this commuter town. People were evacuated; trains stopped; disposal experts did their careful work. These fragments emerge from time to time, as if to remind us where we are. As we walk, I can't stop thinking about this. Even on days this bright, the landscape doesn't let you forget.

The railway bridge we're crossing is one of these fragments, built by the GDR in the 1950s to bypass West Berlin. Without it, the Wall might not have been possible. It is long, reaching across the width of the lake, which on a day this hot looks more like a small sea. Like the Great Lakes I grew up with, it is scaled for sailboats, not swimmers. The long walk in this heat hasn't helped; I have decided in advance, unfairly, petulantly, that this lake is no good.

The small break in the trees that eventually presents itself is actually quite fine. The powder black remains of a camp-fire sit near the water, which edges in gentle waves along the sand. Stepping in, I find the sand stretches a long way out, flat and shallow, and I swim out a way. Twenty yards from shore, I can touch the bottom. It isn't as bad as I'd expected, but there's no wilderness here, nothing to overwhelm and nothing to surprise. It feels safe, like the lake isn't actually the small sea I'd thought it was, but merely a re-wilded expanse of swimming pool. Artificial blue and without life, just us paddling by the shore, a party boat nearby, and a small child and father a few yards away, splashing one another.

*

Swimming pools were the sites of so many of my memories. In one, I was eight, and my parents had decided that I needed to learn to swim properly. I'd not been back to the YMCA since the foam duck incident, but I'd developed an excitement for the water, a love of swimming. So on Monday nights Mom and I drove to the YMCA and took joint, private swimming lessons, like siblings or best friends. We would listen to Phil Collins on cassette tape in the car and after our lessons we would buy plastic-wrapped Black Diamond cheese slices and egg-salad sandwiches from the canteen. Mom was an ally, a secret-keeper. I was the youngest, the baby.

Like me, she didn't know how to swim. But she was a grown-up so it took her longer to learn, and by the time I was learning the sidestroke – arms and legs joining and jutting outwards like an off-kilter frog – Mom was just blowing bubbles in the shallow end, her prescription goggles fogging in the water.

The teacher sent me out to swim laps while Mom practised floating, her legs sinking low into three and a half feet of water. We were in the twenty-five-metre-lane pool, and through the glass window by the deep end I could see the big, square, retractable-bottomed diving pool. We never went in there, and I was okay with that.

The lessons were always the same. Mom and I would put on our swimsuits – mine was silver, my favourite colour that year – and slip on our flip-flops and pad on to the pool floor. We would leave our glasses with our towels, so neither of us could see properly. Mom's vision had always been worse than mine, so my image of her swimming always includes her face squished up beneath thick, black goggles. I could still see fairly well, but I needed to squint to see the huge, round clock with a perpetually moving second-hand tracing the time between eight and eight-thirty. Mom was in the shallow end, her hands on the wall and her face in the water, and I was swimming laps between the lane ropes. The deep end was six feet deep, and when I reached the wall I paused for a minute before taking a deep breath and sliding, pin straight, until my tippy-toes reached the bottom. Monday at eight was rush hour at the pool, so I wasn't scared.

But here's what I was afraid of: sometimes, on a quiet night, I would see the only other swimmers moving towards the pool's edge and I'd realise they were getting out. If they got out, I would be the only person in the water. I would feel my heart bounce into my throat and start swimming as fast as I could, grabbing the wall and heaving my tanned little legs on to the tile. It was not okay to be the only person in the pool.

The year before, when I was seven, I stayed up late watching YTV, when they turned the channel over to the children's horror shows, duplicated in terrifying paperback books at the Scholastic Book Fair. Tucked into the far end of the beige sofa, pyjamaed and clutching my orange blanket, I watched as suburban teenagers were drowned in their high-school swimming pool, pulled underwater by some unseen, wrathful ghost. The pool, I learned, had been built atop an ancient burial ground, and they had neglected to remove one of the bodies.

At eight I could hardly remember the foam duck but the whole haunted pool thing was too much for me. So while I swam laps during swimming lessons and found myself really enjoying swimming and was even quite good at it, I kept an eye out for the telltale signs of being the last one left in the water. Never swim alone, the pool rules said, and I took them very, very seriously.

An early summer heatwave hangs over Berlin, and by the weekend we're all desperate for relief. I'm at no loss for swimming partners in this heat. I haven't seen Tom and Natasha together for months, but we're all here now. It's summer and we're excited.

We take the train east to Kaulsdorf and then loop our way down the suburban streets to find the sun-drenched stretch of grass that borders the Kaulsdorfer Seen. I trace my fingers atop my phone's map, and see three small, blue shapes in a field of green. I see the blue dot telling me we're standing right there, but I can't actually see the lakes yet. I see only fields. Tom takes the lead and trudges forward into the grass and scrub, the brambles high as our shoulders. We're cutting a line through blades of grass that I imagine hold tiny, patient ticks, waiting for blood. I see a swathe of nettles ahead and dig my heels into the ground.

'We can't go that way. I can't go that way.' I'm allergic to nettles, and I don't like ticks, who apparently, I read, can live up to eighteen years awaiting a meal. This fact has refused to leave my brain, and my paranoid legs are beginning to sting in the grass. 'We need to go around the field.'

But Tom isn't listening. He's twenty feet ahead, parting the scrub with his fingers and taking us into a copse of trees. Sighing, I run forward, and Natasha follows me close behind until we're hunched down, avoiding branches spread atop the dank ground. There are voices on the other side of the wood. The red and orange of someone's T-shirt flash past, and I can see it now: a path running along the opposite end of the trees. I can hear the water now too, splashing and laughter streaming in from somewhere just out of sight. I step out in front and forge a path through the branches, emerging dazed and temporarily blinded on to a well-trodden field path. There's a lake at its end.

Glancing at my map again, I see that this is Butzersee, not the lake we're headed for but part of the same nature reserve reclaimed after sand and gravel quarries left the area in the 1930s. Many of the lakes in Brandenburg were formed by glaciers, but a good number are the remains of sand pits, clay pits, gravel quarries and lignite mines. These anthropogenic lakes are among the clearest: sand-bottomed and silken. Clear to the bottom, even from a distance, the bright emerald lakes in Kaulsdorf are fed with ground water, and the nature reserve here serves to protect that. The local community gets its water here, and as we round the end of Butzersee and make for Habermannsee, where we plan to swim, the sense that this is a local lake becomes even more prevalent.

A field of tall grass scattered with sorrel and buttercup stands between the lakes, and between the blades of grass stand half a dozen naked, sun-browned men, hands on hips, penises like cockles sewn beneath their bellies. We pass them by as we approach the white sand that edges Habermannsee, and as we arrive at the lake we find it equally well-populated by naked families, all speaking

German, and clusters of teenagers huddling around stereos blasting techno. Litter overflows from bin bags lashed to trees around the site. I feel as if we have stumbled into a scene, scripted and staged, that shouldn't include us. There are now so few places in Berlin where English-speakers don't belong that I am momentarily surprised, but we press on, self-consciously, quietly.

There's a small island ahead, reached only by slipping off our shoes and walking knee-deep across the lake, and here we settle on a small beach. The beach is lined with fast-growing bamboo, and young birch trees stand in reminder that this isn't an old place. The foliage is stark, sun-drenched and uncharacteristic for Brandenburg. I strip off and move out into the lake, tiny carp darting around its shallows, and I swim underwater to the lake's middle. I want to swim to the bottom, as if I might find something of magic. I think of the German fairy tale of Rübezahl, who hid gemstones at the bottom of a clear fountain to capture his lover. I've never seen water this clear – I can just about see the lake floor – like some tropical sea had been dropped into the middle of suburban Germany. We stay a long while, until the sun dips low at the tree-tops, and I think at the time that it is the best day of summer.

'There are, for the lover of nature, days which are worth whole months.' William Wordsworth wrote this in his guide to the Lake District, and though I've more often taken to reading his sister, Dorothy, I have had these days, and they have stretched and contracted in my memory of that time.

My earliest days in Berlin were wet, with heaving downpours on hot afternoons, quick and unexpected. And they were bright – pink and alight with sunsets fiercer than I'd seen before. The late summer came with clarity, the air refined, the skies more vivid. Occasionally I think this is the fanciful work of memory, but I have photographs, and they are all affected with this quality.

Of course, there has always been something in swimming – in water – of ritual. Water blessed and scattered on the forehead, water to cleanse, and water to convey the ashes in death – the medium on which we are carried and given to the world. So in beginning to swim in Weißer See every week, it seemed natural that Jacob and I undertook it as if it were sacrament. We never missed a swim, though there was no solemnity in it. For months, we swam with a joy found only in the weightlessness of water.

We began on the frayed edge of summer, in that uneasy period in September when it is warmer in the water than the air, the sun still falling in golden swathes of light, the last gleam of an ember. The fountain – which for the past hundred years has remained a palmate jut of white water – wasn't flowing, a sure sign that swimming season was meant to be over. The park attendants watched, unamused but unconcerned. The contrariness of our swimming was half the appeal, I think. Punk in reverse, a friend once called it.

It was the first of those swims, and we were in the middle of the lake and swimming towards the fountain. The fountain wasn't doing anything in particular, just floating on an anchored raft a hundred yards from shore. An island on the horizon to fix our gaze upon, the fountain gave us something to do. We breast-stroked towards it, half-racing and half-transfixed in conversation. Once we were upon it, we paused.

All morning, our words had arrived freely and been thick with meaning. But when we pushed off from the fountain and made for shore, Jacob caught my eye for only an instant, and in that impetuous glint of blue light, there was no sound. For a moment, I was breathless. My words couldn't meet it, so I submerged myself instead, breaking his gaze with the water that held us afloat. *Lakes carry us into recesses of feeling otherwise impenetrable.*

That instant and the concentric waves I left on the surface dissolved, written only in water. We never spoke of it. But in that moment, the centre of gravity in my life changed. Jacob broke through the surface of my steady solitude, settling into that uneasy, turbulent space between friendship and love. From then on I wanted nothing more than the time we spent together. And I remember each of our swims together with the clarity and elasticity that only belongs to those particular kinds of days, the days worth ages.

I've made a mistake, I think, in putting the best lakes at the beginning. I've been plucking my favourites from the Excel spreadsheet of lakes I've catalogued with notes on how to get to them, when I should go, and what each lake is like. The list has grown to eighty-six lakes, far more than I can manage. I've naturally settled on familiar lakes to begin with.

It's only just the end of June and we're on our way to Liepnitzsee, and I worry the rest of summer, not to mention the coming winter, will be dire. My moods – momentarily alive and then bleak again – are growing tiresome, swaying unpredictably by the day. But I want to share this doughnut-shaped lake, left by glacial retreat, with my Canadian friends before they leave town. Berlin is a city of comings and goings, and you learn to make the most of the time you have. We've brought doughnuts, thinking we were being funny.

Last December, I swam here through a thin fog as a light snow melted from the trees. Winter had barely touched the city, but the water breathed like dry ice into the atmosphere. My best friend Rachel, who had flown across the world to see me before Christmas, stood on the shore taking photos, supervising me with a quiet combination of worry and wonder. It was one of the best days I'd had in a long time. Now it's summer, and the light is falling between the beech leaves and the forest is warm. I miss Rachel – struck by that feeling of wanting the only other person you've been somewhere with to be there always – but I know this group of friends will be moving on soon, and then I'll likely be swimming alone.

On a weekend Liepnitzsee is inundated, but it's Thursday so we have it mostly to ourselves. I lead them to the small wooden dock midway across the lake, and as we arrive I see it is occupied by a sunbathing, corpulent and naked man, so we back-track and find the next opening in the trees. It's shaded at the water's edge, but ten feet out the sun cuts a line across the water, and the lake shines turquoise and clear. We swim a while, everyone marvelling at the lake's clarity and the extraordinary contrast with the slate-coloured water of Canadian lakes, before retreating to shore and eating our modest picnic. I've promised the group a hike, so we pack up quickly and set off into the woods.

A small hill rises over the lake-side, and we get one final glimpse of the water before turning north and into the trees. The stretch of Brandenburg north of the city is all forest in my mind; thick beech-wood and winding paths, which eventually outlet into pinewoods that, by all accounts, could only belong to the cultural imagination of this part of the world. The air is thick with sappy pine, and we're confronted with a wall of branches, impenetrable as dark fairy-tale thorn.

I know there's a path here so I forge ahead towards it, but my friends remain frozen in place. They've never seen anything like it; every children's story brought to life before their eyes. I'm dragging them into the pinewood, without a crumb trail to leave behind. The doughnuts are gone. But these dense pine forests appear only in patches, I promise them, most of the forest lopped for timber; these dense stands are but short stories in the landscape, and on the other side we'll find our train back into town.

landing

The Canadians have left town now, as most people do, and I'm stood alone on the miry edge of Flughafensee – Airport Lake, another remnant of Berlin's quarries – watching the planes take off. The water is repellent, sludge green and being policed by a family of swans. Resentment wells to the surface; I don't want to swim here.

I can see a pair of women training for something out in the middle of the lake. I know the water's fine, but the reality of having committed myself to a ridiculous plan has finally materialised in the form of this disgusting bird swamp. For months, I've been reading homemade websites and local forums extolling the joys of Flughafensee. But here, a coil of soaked, filthy cotton rots on the beach; hooks that are the necks of waterbirds skim through the green. I walk a furious loop around the shore and back to the spot by the swans, who have begun harassing a teenaged couple kissing on a nearby bench.

I toss my bag on to the sand and undress, stepping into

the shallow muck and swimming out. The water's better farther out, but I've decided not to enjoy it. I hook my fingers into anger as if on to a cliff's edge; there's no saving today's swim.

The pool rules said never to swim alone. Don't swim immediately after eating. No running. There were rumours that the pool's water would turn purple if you peed in it. At summer camp as a child, the sign said: 'Welcome to our ool. Notice how there's no P in it? We'd like to keep it that way.' These rules were sacrosanct: at the neighbourhood pool I spent my childhood summers in, we knew that if we broke the rules we would be swiftly reprimanded by the local nosy parkers. So I spent most of my time counting laps, swimming the pool end to end underwater, practising something akin to a dolphin's tail stroke. Missy, my new best friend from Missouri, raced me across the pool and spent the summer teaching me a gymnastic, underwater wheelbarrow, she upside down, clasping my ankles as I clasped hers. Entire days were spent on this one feat of aquatic brilliance, broken only at lunch-time when we would run home to eat Lunchables on the screen-porch. I was nine and Missy was ten, so she got to be in charge. I memorised her house rules for Uno and Monopoly, and began to pronounce the word 'towel' with a Midwestern accent. *Taaal*.

  We were best friends every summer and every Christmas, when our families packed up and moved to Florida for the holidays. In Canada, people like us were called Snowbirds, flying south for the winter. But we spent our entire summers there too, so I grew used to being American for a few months, riding my bike up the numbered streets and buying blue raspberry slushies from the Circle K. I didn't really know what the difference was between Americans and Canadians, but the other kids at the pool asked me about penguins and igloos. And they were really confused by my dad's British accent and my Chinese mom; like I should have been able to articulate who I was simply, to melt it into one thing. Missy didn't care, though, so we spurned the other kids and colonised the deep end of the pool, rating each other's dives and seeing who could hold their breath underwater the longest. We lived in swimsuits and oversized T-shirts.

Our summers stayed like this for what felt like many years. At twelve, though, my parents divorced, and I think Missy's parents wondered if I would be a bad influence. The summers after that, they encouraged us to go to youth club at the Baptist Church down the road, and I went until eventually it felt as if the joy that held Missy and me together couldn't be found again. It wasn't about her, I knew, but about the fact that spending the afternoon practising our best underwater tricks no longer fixed things. Inside the pool gates, the rules could only keep us safe for a while.

Later in the week, I try again, deciding to leave Berlin and head into the woods alone. A long walk, I think, might fix my mood. And a long swim might even make me happy. I board the S-Bahn and take it east to the end of the line, then walk the suburban mile and a half to the forest in Strausberg. I know this forest reasonably well, having hiked it the previous Boxing Day, when a thick, sticky snow lined the pines and dripped on to the icy paths.

Returning in summer, I find it profoundly changed, with resiny sweetness in the air and more oaks and beeches lining the lake's edge. I've only ever seen it in winter.

I decide to swim in Straussee, one of the three lakes in this forest, and follow the packed-dirt path around the lake's eastern edge. A hundred yards in, three young boys are laughing in the shallows as they take turns on the rope swing looped around a tree's branch. I pause and watch them swing for a while, tracing broad arcs in the blue sky before letting go of the rope and falling with graceless splashes into the lake. I never did this as a child, and now, in a way, I want to join them. But the longer I stand here watching, the more apparent it becomes that I'm staring, so I keep walking.

Straussee is enormous: clearings in the trees make spaces for swimmers, but a hundred yards out sail-boats jostle on the light waves. A tiny ferry boat juts back and forth between the landings, dropping day trippers off in the Strausberger and Blumenthaler Wald, an enormous stretch of forest that sits between Berlin and Strausberg. It's Sunday and it should be busy, but a cluster of strato-cumulus clouds have taken up residence in half the sky, so everyone has packed up. I'm delighted.

A thin, gauzy sadness had settled on me this week, but the journey here has already helped turn up the edges of loneliness. Instead, there's solitude. Midway across the lake, I find a long wooden dock and spread my towel at its end, settling down with my legs dangling over towards the water. The conical lines of deep green trees break up the horizon, and I think it looks rather like the view at my parents' cottage back in Canada. After lying stretched in the patchy sunlight, I dive off the dock's edge into the amulet blue, feeling so wholly present in the water that I forget I'm alone, and climb out and jump off again and again until I'm exhausted.

In Ontario, a few hours from home, the landscape is scattered with lakes. It sits beyond the endless coils of concrete and brake lights, running far into the distance, webs that encircle the cities and ensnare those within them. You can only leave the cities if you can navigate past these highways, but beyond them lies this place of wood smoke and riotous colour. The grey of concrete turns to green trees and then grey again, slate and granite. It's broken by blue – the deepest kind, almost black, which only shines if the sky is bright. Breaks in the trees and granite reveal them, dark and glassy and unassuming. On a dull day, it's a place for flannel coats and seeing your breath on the air, but in summer you can dangle your legs into the water, cold against the heat.

I wasn't born into that wild place. I was born into a tangle of identical suburbs, of safe streets and shopping malls containing miniature golf courses. Kerbsides filled with browning December slush that stayed there until March. I remember being in cars – pinned to the seat by a seat belt stretched over my pink snow-suit or legs stuck to the leather in summer – and at gas stations, parking lots and traffic lights. The Canada on the back of our coins – loons and moose and trees and waste – wasn't here. It was out there: beyond the traffic on the 401 and impenetrable. We believed it was there, a wilderness into which we were all born, safely kept behind the strip malls and drive-through doughnut shops. It was a half-truth we grew up with. You come to Canada and become Canadian – as if the wild is pumped intravenously into the newly arrived. We never talked about what was really there: poverty and bad water and the lives of entire places erased. That was the invisible, impenetrable wild beyond the city. Once in a while, I'd be shuttled along the highways to lake-fronts that showed the Canada on our coins. What was in between, I never got to know.

I was thirteen, and my dad and stepmother had taken us along the highway to the cottage near Georgian Bay, a great swathe of cold water north of Lake Huron. It was set on to a rocky ledge backed by forest, and we could only get there by motorboat. After spending summers in Florida, the Canadian tradition of long weekends in Cottage Country was new to me, and I didn't like it a bit. There were mosquitos and spiders and probably bears. There was an enormous black lake, but there was nowhere I was brave enough to swim.

I hated everything at thirteen; with a combination of perfectly timed angst and bookishness, I had predictably decided to spend the weekend reading Aldous Huxley in the corner. My older sister and my new step-siblings went swimming in the lake. I wanted nothing to do with it.

We were being introduced to my stepmother's parents – our step-grandparents – who welcomed us into their family with the matter-of-factness available only to Europeans who have lived through a war. There was no fuss made there; you prayed before dinner and you ate what was cooked for you. In the early evening, you went fishing. Nick, 'Grandpa', was probably the nicest, most straightforwardly kind man I've ever met, but there was a lump in my throat and I had nothing to say. I had barely seen my own mother in months, and now I was meant to be making nice with my new family. Nick was inviting me fishing, inviting me swimming, and looked genuinely heartbroken when I turned him down.

Nearly two decades later, this devastates me. There is little to be done for the anger of a thirteen-year-old girl whose parents have just divorced, but for this incredibly kind man who wanted only to show me this place by the lake that mattered so much to him, I still feel a persistent kernel of guilt. That same year he would take us fishing for our dinner, and in my steely stubbornness I would insist that he put the poor fish back. The gap in understanding between us seemed impassable; I wouldn't let anyone cross it.

Now, the sun is waning in the sky at Straussee, and I've dried off fully on the dock. There's a snack hut nearby, so I pack up my bag and wander over, closing the rusty gate behind me. Inside, I find a kindly middle-aged man standing behind an ageing chip-board counter-top, fiddling with a radio. I haven't talked to anyone all afternoon, but when he greets me and asks how my day has been, the words rush out like water.

I order french fries and, at his insistence, an *Eisschokolade*, which he delivers to me ceremoniously, its powdery chocolate milk crowned with whipped cream and a pirouline biscuit. He presents it with a smile that speaks of such pride in his work that something in my solitude shifts. We stand, chatting a while in broken German.

The forest at Strausberg is protected land, cut through with paths for hikers and scattered with the occasional hunting blind. There isn't much else here after the old town ends and the lake begins. In the forest, I remember only pines. But this man with greying hair and a starched apron is telling me about this place: about the boat he crosses the lake with every day to get to work, and about his cabin in the woods, across the water. Until the nineteenth century there were wolves in this forest, and this man – who is watching me eat this *Eisschokolade* with delight – lives there now.

I think about the places I've lived: the tiny apartments in Nova Scotia, London, Toronto, Berlin, and about this man's cabin in the most beautiful forest I know, and leave the snack hut with the most incredible gratitude for this man, and for my paltry German.

baptismal

July hangs heavily in the air, and work days are spent inside pressed near the window, longing for full sun. A weary combination of discipline and deadlines keeps me inside, aglow by the laptop light, writing about metropolitan enclosures in nineteenth-century London, so far away from the German city outside my studio's plate-glass window. I spend the entire day writing about the history of Hampstead Heath for my doctorate, but at lunch-time I step briefly into the sun and wander in a stunned haze over Tempelhofer Feld. Its dormant airfields are carpeted with rough meadow grass and sorrel, and I stand watching the kites amassed like airlift parachutes in the sky. There is sadness here, but brightness too. In a few weeks' time, the airport will be converted into ramshackle, makeshift refugee accommodation.

By evening, away from my desk again and on my green bicycle, I race home to Prenzlauer Berg, sneaking a glimpse of the Fernsehturm glinting on the horizon north of the Oberbaum Bridge. Somehow, Toronto seems closer, and London too, within sight of a tower stretching high. The tiniest parcels of homesickness for places I've left dissipate beneath the Fernsehturm. A city becomes home by these markers; every city has a tower.

The days are all like this, a rhythm of work and travel broken only by my swims. At times, I feel that the work is all I have, but I'm annoyed by the melodrama of that thought. Besides, the lakes are there, calling.

It's Tuesday. Biking on, I pass my turning home and race past Prenzlauer Berg, up into Weißensee, the evening sun at my back. The market stalls at Antonplatz are beginning to pack up, and I remember those occasional mornings when Jacob and I stopped here for eggs or bread for breakfast. I remember the morning after a swim, when we came for vegetables, and the fruit-stall lady forced me to try a quince. I hesitantly but politely brought its milky sweetness to my mouth, and Jacob laughed, discreetly taking it from me, eating it himself. He was forever saving me from wasting fruit, taking my half-eaten apples when I'd grown tired of eating them, trading me half-full thermos cups of coffee to share. But today, I bike past the market and past Weißer See itself, thoughts of those days rising and falling lightly as breath. The evening is hot and smells of warm grass, and I want to swim.

A mile on, a gravel road opens on to Orankesee, an unknown patch of clear water so near to home. That I've never swum here seems absurd, its figure-eight of tree-lined lake just fifteen minutes from my flat, so much brighter than Weißer See. Swimming in Weißer See had become a habit, and coming here now on my own is part of the process of breaking it. I lock my bike to a rusting street sign and follow the path to the lake's edge, across the grassy shore and away from the crowds of splashing children. There is a group of grey-haired swimmers tracing lengths near the wooded shore, so I step into the water there. It's clean sand all the way out, not a single rock or bottle cap or sink-hole of muck. For months, I'd come so close to here; Orankesee feels like starting anew.

My parents were used to my stubbornness and my fear. When I gave up eating fish at six – proclaiming that I'd be a marine biologist and save all fish everywhere – they eye-rolled and left me to it, joking that I would have to get in the water first. It was neither the first nor the last of such moral stands, the kind only the very young and the very stubborn have the will to see through. My rigid refusal to step into the lake or into the ocean may have frustrated them, but it was never a surprise.

Their divorce some years later would change so much, and I would spend the decade after it unearthing its debris. Anger and despair and silence. But I know now there were glimmers of love amidst the grey: their panicked figures at the YMCA pool window, moments spent singing 'Summer Holiday' in the car on road trips, before they would fight and before the police would pull us over for speeding. These were the shining gemstones at the bottom of the lake.

A summer week in 1995, when I was eight, we drove north towards Temagami, a town with one clapboarded Chinese-Canadian restaurant and a wharf of two-storey house boats with blue water slides curling down their backs. My sister Nika was doing a summer exchange with a girl from Wiesbaden, Germany, and her exchange partner Nadja was with us. She brought Germany into our lives; I didn't realise then how important that would be.

In the town, my mother, Nika, Nadja, and I stopped for fried rice and chicken – Mom quietly criticised the food, but I loved its sticky sweetness – while Dad handled the boat rental. It was a small boat – a hideous box suspended on water, seats that turned into beds for us kids, a room in the back for my parents. The roof was a sun-deck, plastic chairs scattered across it and a small bucket fastened to a string at the top of the blue slide.

It was one of the only summers we spent in Canada – I'd been at YMCA day camp in the weeks beforehand, swimming in a concrete-lined outdoor pool in a cartoonish leopard-print bathing suit, and spent the rest of the summer mucking out horse stalls and chasing the cats at the local stable. Now we were up north, a place we came to so rarely, meeting our family friends for a week on the lake, two house boats rented, two dads in sailors' hats trained briefly to captain them. It was a rare moment when our family felt so fully Canadian – play-acting at woodsmanship, singing camp-fire songs in rounds.

The week passed languidly. Our friends had five kids, and they and Nika and Nadja leapt into and out of the water, slight streaks of blond hair careening down the slides and clambering back to the flat roofs of the boats. I stood by the railing, staring at the lake. I had never seen something so dark – a thick, slate-coloured darkness, broken only by the black silhouettes of sunken pine logs. Shadows underwater, they moved with the light at the lake's surface, great hulking figures in the depths. How and why anyone would want to swim near them – these dark bodies that sheltered beasts at the bottom of the lake – baffled me. I stood in the summer sun, watching the others slide and scream and splash.

My parents didn't worry about me. They told me to swim every so often, mocked my stubbornness, reminded me that I was missing out, but experience had taught them there was no forcing me. The cavernous gap between the other kids and me – their willingness to let go and swim, and my complete terror that they should do so – rested there for the week, closed only in the evenings when we would anchor near some remote island, gathering around the camp-fire singing 'The Great Big Moose' and roasting marshmallows to sandwich with chocolate and biscuits for s'mores. Our parents carried on whatever semblance of grown-up conversation was possible with eight children in tow, batting off the mosquitos that joined us at dusk. I fiddled absent-mindedly with the sugared end of my marshmallow-roasting stick, the glowing tip of which kept falling off in the flame.

It was late in the week, the northern summer at its hottest, when it happened. That small glimmer I keep closed in hand, when my father's love was most real and fierce and unequivocal, and when he terrified us the most. Seven kids are in the lake and on the boat, leaping off its sides and looping from ladder to slide. I'm at the railing, watching them go, and Dad is standing next to me, quietly coaxing me into the water. I'm thinking about getting in, dipping a toe and slipping into the black, terrifying deep.

Then, from the sky, from the boat deck above me, the

lake is pouring down. Cold and wet, I'm screaming. And to the boat's bow, my father is storming. Someone had dumped a bucket of water on my head.

'Which one of you goddamned kids did this?'

It is silent. No one wants to step forward. The empty bucket, secured with twine, swings from the upper railing. The summer heat freezes over.

And then, in disbelief and discomfit, my father's friend – the other dad on the trip – steps forward, admitting that he meant it as a joke. He thought it might help me get in the water. My father is raging, swearing, arms waving. I hear only snippets, *How dare you*s, reproaches, and apologies.

We've all seen this rage before, but now, in this one glowing moment, it's about me. My dad is defending me, turning on his friend for me. And I know instantly that somewhere in this anger is love – so much of it – and I'll continue to hold it close, a talisman of a memory, saying, *Take your time, it'll be okay,* whenever I go near a lake again.

By the end of July I've worked up some nerve. Swimming for six weeks has taken its effect: a strengthening of patience, a willingness to spend long days alone. If Orankesee had righted me, a long swim might give me momentum.

I spend the train ride in memory – grasping at amorphous memories of a train ride in winter – holding my bike upright amidst the Sunday crowds. I heave it off at Königs Wusterhausen, checking my map before bouncing along a cobbled road towards the west. I have a plan: there are three lakes on my list. A dull, rain-grey patch of clouds is clearing ahead of me.

The landscape south of Berlin is an unrolling flatness. Parallel rows of green are stitched together with wooded seams, with occasional pines interrupting their agricultural weave. The air smells of manure and pine resin and hay, and sometimes there's a distant, peaty whiff of marsh. Here more than anywhere Berlin's dampness shows itself: the swamp, flat and wet and so shallow the city has to run water pipes above ground from construction sites. It is cobbled and invisible in town, but out here it feels as though gravity has drawn the wetness downwards, like the map had been stood upright and the lakes had fallen south. It's a land of fields that speak of water, even when you can't see it.

Eight kilometres in, I think I'm lost. I've followed the curving weft of the road and passed the sign marking Teltow-Fläming, which I know is the edge of today's territory. Motzener See is somewhere nearby – I can smell it – but I can't see anything but sorrel and poppies and ramshackle cabins ahead of me. I pull to the side of the road and give up, checking my phone.

Somewhere in the past kilometre, I've taken a wrong turn, so I back-track a while. And then, round a bend there's a tree-lined avenue marking the beginning of Kallinchen, a one-street town with a campsite and park running along the lake's edge. I lock my bike at the park, and glancing upwards, notice that the rainclouds have hung around.

I swim quickly, lolling briefly in the toffee-coloured water, before downing a hard-boiled egg and a piece of bread, packing up and moving on. Pätzer Hintersee is six kilometres away, and if I bike fast enough I might find shelter in the pinewoods surrounding it. The road opening ahead is swathed in gold – stormy sunlight filtered through thick cloud. It begins to spit warm rain.

I round the bottom edge of Motzener See and head for the lane leading towards Pätz, but I find instead that the asphalt road turns briefly to sand and then to the rumbling slabs of concrete which form a logging road. The flatness of the land has broken, and ahead of me rises two kilometres of hill through dense stands of pine. It's the fastest and only way through.

I heave up through the growing rain, which makes the dry pined hilltops warm with sticky sweetness, the smell of burnt orange and green. Reaching the hill's apex, I career downwards without pedalling, thumping over the gaps in the slick, chalky concrete of the makeshift road. Halfway down, I hear my bike chain drop.

Furiously, I stop and repair it, black grease coating my fingers, and curse the goddamned map that took me this way. I apologise to my bicycle. There had to be a better way. I should have brought more than my phone. The road ahead turns to trail, and then sand, and then I have to walk.

The white sand grows deeper as I follow the trail through the pines, and eventually the rain abates. But I've been out for hours and am nowhere near carrying out my plan. Three lakes. What was I thinking? I check my phone, but its battery is dead.

My bike squeals and shudders as I push it through the sand. The neat rows of Scots pine turn into clumps of young, scrabbly wood, which linger into scrub and tussocks of tall brown grass. I'm not lost, but neither am I convinced I'm going the right way.

And then, ahead of me, I see three children amidst the grass. One, the oldest, is standing sentry at the path's edge, while the other two, a boy and a girl who can't be more than six years old, are crouched collecting wildflowers and leaves. I scan the horizon; there's nothing but forest and field to be seen.

'*Wolltest du hierhin?*' the oldest one asks, eyeing me suspiciously. Did I mean to come here? What kind of question is that? I don't see what she has to be suspicious about – from what I can tell, she knows this place, and I've just wandered in here and found a group of children alone in the middle of a field of wildflowers. *I* should be suspicious, I think, but I put on my best, most confident self.

'*Ja!*' I chirp. I tell them I'm going to Pätzer Hintersee, at the top of this sandy moor.

'But you're in Groß Köris,' she replies dryly. Her pale brown hair is laced with blades of hay.

I point to the trail ahead and nod enthusiastically, as if I'd known where I was all along. The other children have stopped gathering flowers now, and are stooped in the sand staring at me.

'Where did you come from?' she asks, stepping around me like an interrogator. The other kids have gathered around my bike now, clutching floral clusters in their dusty fingers.

'Berlin,' I say, and before I can continue she is smiling, nodding, saying that they too are from Berlin. But she doesn't offer any explanation for their being here, alone in the middle of nowhere. I realise I've started walking, some distant childhood instinct not to talk to strangers kicking in, though I know full well I'm the adult here. But something about them – her forthrightness, the smallness of the younger boy crouched low to the ground, the fact that I haven't seen another person or a house in miles – puts me off, and I make my excuses, knowing I'm running far behind in my plans. I take the path into the woods, leaving the children and the moor behind.

Ten minutes into the dark green, looking back occasionally, I find the lake – marshy and brown and uninviting. It's a nature sanctuary, and in the quietude nature has run its course, reclaiming the swampy borders of the lake with rotting wood and reed grass. I won't swim. Tiny blue dragonflies skim the water's surface, and I remember reading that there are *Drosera* here – sundews – carnivorous flowers tipped with sticky, pink dew. I don't see them, but the thought of them unsettles me. I feel compelled to back-track, on to the drier part of the trail and away from the lake. The forest track alternates sand and pine needle, its sloping side falling into marsh. A mile or so along, I reach the forest's end.

Checking the town's notice board and map, I see that I've made it to Pätz, a small town south of Königs Wusterhausen. I know I'm not far from the train. But I've only swum once, so I stop quickly at the town's strip of park, edging Pätzer Vordersee. It's windswept and dull, but as I undress an elderly couple emerge from across the road, bare-footed and bath-robed, carrying towels. They leave their robes on the children's playground and step out into the lake ahead of me. Flatly, they launch into the waves, silent the whole time. They don't take any notice of me, so I swim out a few yards away from them, floating on my back, before returning to shore and gathering my things, exhausted. I'm angry with myself. *Too ambitious, too disorganised. I don't know what I'm doing.*

The signpost in town tells me I'm ten kilometres from the train station, so I set off on the paved shoulder, defeated, finding my bike rhythm again. I'm a few minutes in, trance-like and longing for home, when a plate of turquoise, glassy water flashes from the roadside. I brake, shuddering into the gravel. And here is the thing I'd wanted all day – clear and glassy, blue and cool, a clay pit reclaimed as a lake. It is quiet and small, without a breath of wind, appearing out of nowhere. I thrust my bike against a tree and am in, tank-top soaked through, swimming to its centre. Redemption.

marking time

At twenty-eight, I feel a shimmering glimpse of excitement when I call my dad on the phone. It's something I didn't do for so long that now, when I feel excited to call and let him talk at me about home renovations or cycling or rugby, I think it's a small gift I received by accident. I never planned to be the woman who called her dad on the phone every week any more than I planned to be the woman who *didn't* call, and who moved incredibly far away on purpose, who got married at twenty-three despite her family's disapproval and then had to work out how to get a divorce without hearing the words *I told you so*. But having been both, I now find a small thrill in wanting to call home.

Dad's at the cottage when he answers, and for a moment I'm struck by how much he's beginning to answer the phone like my grandfather did. A booming, swinging 'Hello' that makes me imagine he is scooping up a very heavy receiver attached to a rubbery coil, but then there's his tinny FaceTime voice on the end of the line. I quickly search for a reason to have called, dropping in something about visiting home, and then the conversation continues as usual, with him updating me on his cottage chores like it's stock-market ticker-tape, essential news. I didn't call for any reason in particular, other than that I've been living with this amorphous ball in my stomach, some unidentifiable and unspecific longing for familiarity. Homesickness, maybe, but I'm no longer quite sure what it is that I miss or where home is. His updates momentarily fill that space. I'm silent on the line, adding only the occasional *Mhmm*.

The rest of the time, I fill my days at work or on my bike, hot summer rushing into my lungs. I've been making lists of full-day lake trips to take before summer is out, and today is another. I've promised Terresina, who is just passing through Berlin for the summer, a day of lake swimming.

We follow the busy road from Erkner towards the east to a string of skinny lakes connected by small canals, a chain of lakes designed for boats. We ride to the end of the chain, Möllensee, and lock our bikes in the woods before continuing on foot past forest benches and quiet campsites. At the far end of the snaking coil of lake, we stop and swim. It's green – the water dense with clouds of algae and leaf – but as we swim out, it becomes clearer. Terresina tells me she's never really swum much in lakes, and we bob and roll on the water's surface, commiserating about our fear of deep water as small boats chug by. Underwater, I see her tattooed legs blur and shift in the moving water and I think, momentarily, that it's one of the most beautiful things I've seen. I won't see this again.

On shore again, I tear a pretzel in half and we eat, digging our toes into the sand. And then, as quickly as we came, we're on our bikes again, heading to the other end of the lake chain, Werlsee. Here, we swim farther out, even more boats moving nearby, and then retreat to the hut by the beach for soft ice cream, sitting crossed-legged and curling our mouths over the tight whip of chocolate and vanilla. She'll be gone in a few weeks. These friends in Berlin come and go.

Leaving Terresina, I'm reminded of a day last year. It was October, and Jacob was looking at me suspiciously.

'You're only here for a few months,' he said before turning back to his cup of coffee. We'd been swimming for nearly a month, meeting on the corner by the church and biking to Weißer See in the early morning. Afterwards, over coffee, we'd talk or argue or sit in quiet company with one another. Today was an argument.

'I may come back.'

He looked unconvinced. 'Everyone says that.'

A few weeks earlier, we'd walked around Mitte in Berlin's centre, tracing a lingering route down Linienstraße and down along the Spree, and he'd described the orphan sensibility of young Berliners and the city's many temporary residents. Everyone leaves, he had told me, so you try not to get attached. I'd laughed, then, but now, when he was using it to push me away, it seemed a barbed and prophetic remark. I wondered if our days together were just marking time.

*

If you've ever counted the rings on a tree stump, you have a sense of the way the landscape holds its own history; the way time recedes beneath the surface of the ground. Sand, gravel and rock layered year by year. Ice is layered just the same – glaciers hold their ages in their cores.

Tree rings, pollen samples and the ground strata have all helped to shape the story of glaciation in Brandenburg. In the middle of the twentieth century, scientists began using radiocarbon dating to determine the age of geological formations. The middle of the twentieth century – 1950 – was established as the stable scientific marker of the present. The landscape of Brandenburg was most profoundly transformed in the Weichselian glaciation, beginning over a hundred thousand years before 1950.

In the middle and later periods of the Weichselian glaciation, ice advanced southward from Scandinavia, pushing past the Baltic and over the north of Germany. When a glacier moves across a landscape, it picks up ground strata along the way, moving rocks from their places, carving up the land beneath the ice. The ice sheets of the Weichselian extended hundreds of kilometres inland from the Baltic, reaching the southern edge of Brandenburg, the edge of the North German Plain. As a result, glacial spillways and plateaus undulate across the landscape, shaped by the movement of the glaciers, moraines scattered by the ice. Eleven thousand years ago, as the world warmed again and the ice retreated, the lakes were left behind.

The time of glaciers seems obscure, too long or too slow to comprehend. It is drastically different from the transformations happening now. Over the past fifty years, lake water has warmed. As distant ice melts at the poles of the world, so too does lake ice disappear. The lakes left behind by glacial retreat tell us something of our warming planet, changes happening faster than ever before, glaciers outpaced. They are markers in time, emergency flares in an advancing crisis. In lakes, the present history of our world contracts and intensifies, urgent and shrinking like the ice.

I take my parents' divorce to be a marker, a line drawn between childhood and adulthood. I doubt this is uncommon. Not that divorce is a bad thing; it was certainly the right thing for my parents and many others, and I don't begrudge them that. For a girl on the cusp of teenhood, there was never going to be a good time.

On either side of the marker, I see things differently, as if before everything changed, things were less my fault, less my responsibility. Afterwards, I am fully formed, adult and responsible. I wasn't even thirteen. But I acquired the hard habit of seeing myself this way, as if in the moment my father explained what was happening, I'd decided to grow up. I lived in their house, but I was on my own.

When my parents decided to divorce – a fact which I absorbed silently before asking if I could go eat my grilled-cheese sandwich – my sister and I ended up living with my dad, remaining in our childhood home. My mother moved to an apartment nearby, and then another, and another. I hadn't seen it coming, hadn't imagined divorce to be a possibility, even in the times my sister and I sat on the stairs, listening to their arguments. I'd never met anyone who was divorced. I didn't know what it meant.

The years after were scattered with legal battles, times apart from one another, calls by my sister and me to crisis helplines as my mother stood locked behind the bathroom door, pill bottles in hand. My parents grew tense and busy with their divorce. My sister and I learned to take care of one another, each coping in our own ways. Mine was retreat.

Everything came unmoored. Mom receded into a world of work and worry, eating thirty-cent ramen noodles instead of the full meals she had raised us on. Her face became haunted, pained. When I was fourteen, she was sent away for a time, and I didn't see her at all. When Mom came home again, she was the mother I'd always known: she cooked again and gave love so fully. But by then I knew what was possible, how it could change.

I resolved not to be like that. That I would be stronger, as if strength were the crux of the problem.

The last summer with both my parents, Mom and I had been collecting plants: orchids and *Tillandsias*, which we'd lashed to the tree trunks in the Florida garden. One afternoon, we had driven to the Selby Botanical Garden and I'd brought home a new clay pot with five openings. I filled each soilless hole with a thin green plant, and placed it proudly at the front door.

A few years after that last summer, I noticed the pot taken over by one of the plants, *Tillandsia aeranthos*, long since being tended, a grey-green spray of leaves with cotton-candy-hued inflorescences. It had been my favourite, and now it had taken over, grown too full for its home. The orchids on the trees had grown thick roots, clutching tightly to the palms, duller than ever, as if they missed being cared for, missed my mother. I was fifteen; I had better things to do.

Instead of swimming and instead of gardening, I had begun staking out the public beach; looking for guys, for new friends – because I wasn't holding on to people for very long at this point – and for some way to pass the afternoons. They charged twenty-five cents for a Styrofoam cup of ice water at the beach, so I scrabbled away my spare change for those afternoons. There was a pastor's son, and the older guys who worked at the surf shop, and a boy from Michigan whose name I had forgotten by the time September arrived. When you're afraid, relationships are a good way to pass the time.

Crushes came and went. With each of them, whether or not they were reciprocated, the space that had opened up around me would be filled. Momentarily, at least, I wouldn't be alone. But all I sought were stop-gap solutions, friends I would keep for a few months, crushes that would dissipate as quickly as they had formed. And in this flippancy, I found that the thing I thought I was most afraid of – being alone and unstable – was the thing I kept choosing.

I didn't care about family. That required consistency. I didn't trust them. But I needed not to be alone, so by the time I was seventeen, I'd come to believe that the thing I needed most was love. Not family. Not friends. I could choose someone to love, and let them love me, and then everything would be okay.

Love was a lot like fear. It swallowed you whole, like water.

an offering

The first entry in the *Oxford English Dictionary* for the word 'lake' doesn't refer to lakes as we know them. Instead, 'lake', from Old English, means 'an offering, sacrifice; also a gift'. This origin of the word has nothing to do with water, but I find myself thinking about it sometimes, about the ways lakes hold themselves open to the world. Broad plates beneath the sky, they welcome a swimmer fully. Perhaps they swallow a swimmer whole. But there's a kind of offering in the generosity of water holding you afloat. In the way water holds feeling, how the body is most alive submerged and enveloped, there is the fullness of grace given freely.

I think of this partly because my time in the lakes has been both gift and sacrifice. The lakes have been centres of both love and loss not solely for me – living in this place, things past and much more significant than me are always present – and they hold those moments stoically, water smoothed to satin. Lakes that have held joy, in time, came to signify incredible sadness, and learning to swim through that, like swimming through feeling, is a part of reinhabiting these places for myself. Much as I've longed for the quietude of places without a past, living here, as much as in Canada or England or anywhere else, it is impossible. There isn't some untrammelled wilderness I can chart. Mühlenbecker See, perhaps more than any other lake, holds feeling in its depths.

I first went there with Jacob, during those early months in Berlin. It was the first days of November, and an unseasonable warmth had spread across the weekend, kaleidoscope trees glowing in a golden sky. Friends had come to dinner and I'd spent the evening cooking curry, furiously and unsparingly, laying out a table for ten. And then, somewhere near the end of the evening, amidst the raucous noise of a card game, Jacob caught my eye and said simply, 'Lake tomorrow?'

We set off early, before the day had settled on the city, and cycled north along Prenzlauer Allee. He rushed ahead on his black bike, putting yards between us, and I pedalled faster, only just keeping up. Away from the city, when we found ourselves alone on one of the country roads lined with silent village houses, he slowed and cycled next to me, chatting about dogs. Australian shepherds. A goose farm appeared to our left, and he joked about Christmas coming soon. I felt only sadness for the birds.

Abruptly, the smooth of the tarmac ended and we were turned on to a sea of ageing cobbles working their way out of the ground as if they had better places to be. Our slender bike wheels slipped in the cracks, hulking and thumping along the quiet road towards the forest.

*

July is nearing its end, and I've worked up some nerve. It's my favourite stretch of forest, despite my memories, and I want to go back. But I want to go back shrouded in safety, with the hands of friends clutched in mine. We're waiting on the train platform at Karow, and Katrin and Lily are talking in a sideways, lost-in-translation way about cars or horses or both. I've lost track. I'm immensely relieved they like one another.

Lily is over from London for just a few days, but I've scrabbled together this encounter on the premise that they're two of my favourites – wild-eyed creatures who belong in a far-away forest but have somehow ended up in these frowning, grey cities. But we all know it's because I was afraid and wanted them to work through it with me. I'm shuffling on the train platform, lifting my heels and shuttling around while they talk.

The blue and white train takes us northward, leaving us at Schönwalde on a lonely, one-sided platform. The forest wraps around it, and as we walk up the mossy dirt track, the trees swallow us in a cathedral of orange and green.

Jacob had been here before. We hopped off our bikes and wheeled them through the uneven dirt track over beech roots and fallen logs. The sky above was veiled in colour, a painted ceiling of oranges from burnt to yellow, flickering like confetti in the warm air. On the ground, it was still.

We stopped at the small, sloping mouth of the lake, blue from the shore. Pausing in the silence, I breathed in the wide expanse of the lake, grassy and warm. The porcelain figures of two white swans slipped into a curve in the shore-line with silent grace. Behind me, Jacob began to undress, and when I turned around he was waiting, naked skin stretched over lithe muscles, unabashed.

'Hurry up!' he chirped and made for the water. I'd packed a swimsuit, but now, with his legs, buttocks, and the curve of his back turned towards me, I felt embarrassed, childish. Slipping out of my clothes, I hugged my breasts and stepped furtively towards the lake. He was in now, splashing and laughing and calling for me, and as I stepped in I sank unexpectedly into the deep. Cold water rising to my waist.

The smell of moss and pine washes over us, though it's been a dry week. I'd hoped for rain, as if the sudden rush of water might bring the forest to life, but it's here all the same, bright and full, but dry. The forest in summer is different from the forest in autumn. Then, the carpets of moss sprout mushrooms, peering through fallen pine needles, cheerful nodes of brown amidst the glowing green. In summer it is just moss, and dry moss at that, no lush floor but flashes of verdancy under fallen logs. Along the path, we come to Schloss Dammsmühle, a castle once commandeered by the Nazis, and then in the GDR by the Stasi. It is still and quiet, its history silent. The salmony paint falls in scales across its turret and the mildewed tile fountain is filled with dead leaf. At the curve of the pond, a tent sits camouflaged in green, three fishermen clad in fatigues, minding their lines. My feet remember the feeling of that pond and the patch of ground where their tents are pitched; I'd sat there last

November, toes dipped into the cold, mirrored water. I lose myself momentarily in that thought. The men look up at us, beer cans pressed to their lips, and track us as we pass, three women in the woods. Katrin and Lily catch my eye, but I'm impetuous. I say hello, and then keep walking, the small thought in the back of my mind that I ought to be more afraid, that I ought to mind my body and my gait, but I don't.

I glance at the pond again and the feeling passes. This crooked wash of brown and blue, once maintained by prisoners from Sachsenhausen concentration camp, will turn to red and gold come autumn. I've seen it; I know this place. But in the moments I get too close, I find it barbed. Himmler was here, and the Stasi. The glimmer of fear I felt passing the fishermen turns to guilt, as though I ought never to have found beauty here, or love.

We swam as long as we could, cold tightening my skin, and then emerged, wet and shivering. On the shore, Jacob wrapped himself in clothes and then watched me dress, five feet away, staring, unmoving. And then, jacket zipped to the neck, he turned and set off back into the forest. Through the brightness of autumn, past the castle and the pond, and into the pine. Two hundred yards in, the rows of pine broke and a path – straight and long and lined with moss – drew us downward. Midway along, a shaft of sunlight lit the ground and we stopped. A single tree had gathered around it a blanket of carpet moss, deep green and aglow, and a glossy brown bolete had curved out of it, so stout I had to lie on my stomach to look at it properly. Jacob sat down next to me, unpacking lunch.

For weeks, I'd cooked or we'd eaten in restaurants, quietly biding our time together, never really acknowledging the feeling growing up between us. But here, on the moss, he spread a chequered towel, cheeses, bread and fruit. He held an avocado in the air, deftly slicing it in half. We ate for a while, warm sun streaming over us, and then folded the picnic away. The sun was still high, mid-way through the afternoon sky, so I shuffled my back towards the pine trunk, legs outstretched. Exhausted, Jacob draped himself over them, head in my lap, and closed his eyes. I moved my fingers through his thick curls, tucking them behind his small left ear with the hesitancy of new touch.

We sat silent, holding, until the sun began to dip. He turned his head half towards me and asked if this was okay. But my heart was already in my throat, in my mouth, out in the air, exceeding me. Feeling had grown down, unfurling its mycelium weave across me as we sat, hooking down under my skin and muscle and limbs. It had climbed down inside me, I'd breathed it in and welcomed it, and held it. I'd held my love out in front of me like an offering, quietly and securely. I knew now, in the broken silence, that whatever I said was just a tiny piece of it, sweet and fleshy on the surface, the feeling already anchored deep inside me. So I said something about patience, and then we climbed up out of the forest floor and rode out, pedalling in time, back to Berlin.

We reach the lake, summer sun blanketing it entirely. Katrin and Lily want lunch, so we spread our picnic out by the shore, legs outstretched in the light. And as they eat, I swim out into the centre, noticing for the first time

Mühlenbecker See's almost molten warmth, the thickness of the water. When I submerge my hands, I can't see them any more, just the colour of the water, gold and bright but never blue. Perhaps it has changed. It's summer and the warmth of the lake tells me how shallow it is.

I roll on to my back and float, sadness rushing off my chest with the water, and then turn to shore. Katrin and Lily wave, smiling, and I smile too, relieved. I make for shore, and there, lunch unpacked, we sit hip to hip, our toes edging the shore. Even now, I can feel the warmth of the summer in my feet.

silk and glass

The lake is so warm I stand there a while, sinking into the ground. Turning my back on the sun, I scan the horizon from the water. From the top of the hill, the Teufelsberg listening station, Epcot-like and crumbling, stares back. I can't see the city, but I know that if I were to climb out and clamber up the winding hillside path, I'd find it off in the distance, still and grey.

The hill suits its name. Teufelsberg means 'devil's mountain'. It was built atop war rubble from the city below. Somewhere beneath the spy station sit the remains of a Nazi technical college. The top of the hill is capped with the station's white domes, covers for the British and American antennae that once searched for signals here. Now, though, the station sits empty, wasting, fenced in. Weeds have grown up everywhere, and the place is a mess of concrete and colour from spray cans. In Teufelsee, though, everything's green – ground and water and forest – so I sink down low, dipping my nose beneath the lake's surface.

When I've finished swimming I dry off on the lawn, hanging my towel over my bike seat to dry. This small pocket of flat land on the hillside catches the sun. The height of the hill above it seems to keep everything else out; my phone lost signal an hour ago. I stay quietly in this green glade.

The weeks after that November day at Mühlenbecker See, Jacob and I sat in a soft, companionable kindness with one another. We ate bibimbap in Korean restaurants and stayed up late watching action movies from the nineties, close and at ease but never touching. In the mornings, we would meet for coffee and plan bike trips, swims, or days on the sofa. He translated the city for me, guided me to unknown lakes, pushed me to venture farther than I might have on my own. With him, I uncovered a kind of vitality that I hadn't known was mine. A liveliness and courage that never factored into the life of books I'd sheltered in. I began to feel bold. I wasn't afraid to swim. In those months, Berlin quickly became home, a steady ground from which I felt less afraid. But the solitude I'd held so securely when I'd first arrived had dissipated; I worried that too much of my feeling of security centred on him.

At the turn of December, we packed our bags and took the train north to the island of Rügen. Tom came with us. We'd planned for a weekend on the Baltic, grey and windswept, and arrived to find it exactly as we'd hoped. East German holiday towns empty in winter as the cold moves in from the north and the waves swell and pound the shingle beaches. I hadn't wanted warmth or sun, but rather the sharp, aspirating air, something to break the monotony of winter.

Sassnitz, at the north-eastern tip of the island, was quiet. Paint peeled off the abandoned city centre, a thick putty-colour plastered over everything. At the waterfront, though, we found our rented apartment, two yellow rooms with a view over the sea, the sound of waves perpetually thrumming on the sea-wall. We stayed inside, where it was warm.

We spent the evening playing improvised games: the boys decided on a form of charades using phrases from the book I was reading and began acting out random words and sentences. It was my turn, and as I sat splayed on the floor – hopelessly acting out Gustave Courbet's painting, *L'origine du monde* – they erupted in laughter. Outside, there was only the black of night and the sea.

In the morning we walked westward, out into Jasmund National Park, the peninsula of land at the edge of Rügen, leaning out over the Baltic. The coast-line here was made most famous, perhaps, by Caspar David Friedrich's paintings, the cliffs and a view of the sea carefully rendered. These eroding chalk cliffs at the edge of the park slip year by year into the sea. Like the lakes in Brandenburg, the cliffs here were carved out by glaciers.

Fontane wrote of Jasmund in his most famous novel, *Effi Briest*. In the novel, the eponymous protagonist – likened to a German Anna Karenina, but younger, more vulnerable – visits the forest at Jasmund with her husband. She is plagued by memories of her own infidelity, and on approaching Hertha See – a round, black lake in the woods – she is overcome by guilt, begs to leave. Hertha

See, I learned, was home to the Slavic goddess Hertha – a kind of mother earth figure – who was said to run through this forest, to bathe in the lake. In some accounts, she was an incarnation of the devil, drowning unsuspecting suitors in the depths of the water. Hertha could only ever be a goddess or a siren. As if the only options for a woman were safety or danger.

Like Effi, we found our way into the forest. Atop the cliffs, there was a spare, winter beech-wood where we walked for hours. Sunlight came down in long, cold shafts, and when we neared the edges of the chalk cliffs, the wind was so strong we had to shout. I sat on the edge, wrapped up but still cold, watching the waves break a hundred metres below.

We walked to Königsstuhl, the 'King's Chair', the highest cliff, and then clambered down the stairs along the white chalk face, towards the sea. Jacob and I wanted to swim. Tom stumbled behind us, cursing the cold, calling us crazy. Standing on the sidelines, he watched us. His face was shocked, dismayed, worried and amused all at once.

On the beach, we tucked into a small cove and undressed. The wind cut like ice. Stepping into the sea, it felt warm; we'd been swimming in lakes much colder than this and I felt powerful. The waves were fierce, though, and as we picked our way over the stones and out into the deep, we had to brace ourselves against them. Great lumbering waves that hit me at my knees, full-force. After five minutes in the water, the feeling left my body. It was too much work, the seabed too rocky, the cold cutting like glass. We stumbled to shore. Back on the beach, looking down, we saw that our feet were covered in blood.

The next day, we went to Prora, to an unfinished monolith of Nazi architecture on the seafront. The concrete buildings ran along the beach for miles, flat-faced, enormous and grim. Intended to be a holiday camp for twenty thousand workers, the buildings were abandoned, bathrooms half-finished, walls half-plastered, windows broken. Cold wind rushed through the openings, into the halls. There were no doors inside. Nearby, developers were remodelling one of the blocks for condos.

Tom needed to sketch the inside of the building as part of a project he'd been at work on, so Jacob and I climbed out through a broken window and went on to the beach. A thin line of pine sat between the buildings and the shore. It was sandy here, but just as windy as the day before.

Alone for the first time in days, we began to talk. Small, quiet words in the wind, so we had to stand close. In that enclosed space – close to one another and in the roar of the sea air – I understood. I was going to leave Berlin soon. It wasn't the right time. I began to cry.

A concrete jetty stood ahead of us, and I clambered out on to it. The wind nearly knocked me backwards, but I walked forward, head ducked against the force of it. I slipped my legs over the edge of the concrete, out over the waves, and sat alone. The water was white, breaking far out from the beach. Waves take their shape from the ocean floor, from what sits beneath them, and they fall only when the balance that sustains their arc-like movement is thrown off, when they reach their breaking point. The energy of the wave is always there, in the water, but it only shows itself when it approaches dry land. These waves – spilling breakers – the kind of waves that result from a slow roll on to land, form far from shore. They roll in slowly, limply, breaking over themselves in a pool of white. They are gradual, steady, undramatic.

Fifty yards out from the jetty, the Baltic broke itself up into white water, and I watched it break. I sat with the grey sea and sky surrounding me, wind draining the moment of sound, crying, wanting the sea to wash all feeling away.

The water at Nymphensee is silk. August has arrived, thick and hot, like July. Summer isn't abating.

I had stepped into the lake and sunken deep into its wet sand, the slippery feeling of quicksand beneath my feet, but now that I'm swimming out to the lake's centre, it is light and soft. I'm not alone – Anne is here, swimming too, and chatting all the while. She's new to me, a fellow writer who has asked to join me for a swim. As we swim out into the lake's middle, talking about the books of Jacob von Uexküll and John von Düffel, I'm convinced she'll be a friend. For now, she swims a few yards away, her blond curls suspended above the water in the periphery of my vision, a bright point at the edge of my sight-line.

Nymphensee is a new lake, man-made, and sits at the edge of Brieselang, a small town west of Berlin. In his *Rambles*, Fontane lamented the changes wrought on the landscape, the turning of marsh into dry land, and being here today, I have a sense of it. There is a dusty dryness; Nymphensee the only patch of water amidst cars and concrete. But the lake itself is sheltered from the roads.

Out of the lake, we settle on the sand amidst the reeds, drinking tea. The forest on this side of the lake is all birch, newly grown after the quarry was closed. The sand around

Berlin is light and fine, and where there is sand, the water seems to share the quality of lightness. In the middle of it, our talk is quiet, gentle.

That's how I remember it. Months later, Anne told me that on the way back we passed a group of neo-Nazis, tattooed and posturing, but naively, I only remember the feeling of the swim, the lightness of the day, the newness of it. Freedom.

Water feels different in each place. The water I grew up with was hard, cutting, and when I go back to visit it now, I feel it in my ears when I dive in. Something different, more like rock. The lake a whetted blade.

The water in Berlin has a softness to it. Maybe it's the sand, buffing the edges off the water like splinters from a beam. It slips over you like a blanket.

There's a safety in this feeling. In the lakes here, there is a feeling of enclosure and security that Canada can't replicate. And it shouldn't – the pelagic vastness there is entirely its own, and I've learned to love that too.

Here, in the middle of the lake, the fear of slipping away dissipates. I'm right in place. I won't slide off the map. I'm at home in the water, and I'm not scared to be alone here.

When I first came to Berlin and began swimming, every moment carried with it a feeling of freedom. It was the first fresh start I'd had in a while, and it was entirely mine. A few years earlier, when I was twenty-four, I'd left a marriage I couldn't fix.

So Berlin held a kind of promise for me. I had mourned the loss of love, found my feet again, and was giving myself the gift of time that I'd not given myself in my early twenties. Back then, I had chosen the temporary safety of a relationship, of a marriage, and the magic of it could only last so long.

Berlin was the first place I had for myself as a woman – I didn't have to be here for anyone but myself, and that was new to me. I felt independent for the first time. On my bike, out in the city, and out in the centre of Krumme Lanke on my own, it felt like the greatest kind of magic. I'd walked away from marriage, from love, and found something incredible in the landscape. In swimming, I'd found a place to be with myself.

And then I met Jacob. I found a kind of bravery swimming with him, a fearlessness I'd longed for. But it came to me in a flood of energy. I wondered if I could ever find that courage on my own. The brief moment of space that had opened up – that gift of time I'd given myself after my marriage – suddenly filled in, wrapped itself tightly around me again. I hadn't learned to love since my husband. I was terrified. I didn't want to give up the space I'd found.

But I did. And afterwards, I was angry.

north

Twenty days before I first moved to Berlin, I sat in the front of my husband's 1998 Toyota Corolla and got a divorce. Actually, that's not quite accurate: I signed the stack of documents – which for months I had referred to as 'the paperwork' – pressed up against the dashboard using a blue ballpoint pen. Five initials and three signatures. I passed them to my left, and he signed them too, an inky blue scrawl.

I had joked repeatedly some years earlier, perhaps at his expense, that he had the most forgeable signature I knew. An abstract squiggle, like two small mountains on a page – I used to forge it all the time. Forgery was the only way to get things done.

But that day, in the Toyota with Nova Scotia plates, I waited. It was hot and he asked me to roll down the window, or maybe it was cold and he asked me to roll it up. I can't remember. It is remarkable to me that I can't remember this small detail from what ought to be an important moment. I remember so much. I remember that there was an enormous, plastic bottle of water in the back seat, the kind you'd buy if you were stockpiling for the apocalypse. He'd always been afraid of tap water. There was an empty, used coffee cup on the floor.

The day before, we had met in the Halifax Public Gardens for coffee, on the benches where we'd spent our early summers swooning and staring into one another's much younger eyes. I was twenty then. Eight years had passed. I'd arrived there early enough to look comfortable, though I wasn't, and had bought myself a cup of coffee on to the lid of which I'd pressed my red-lipsticked mouth while I waited and tried to keep calm. He'd stopped at the gazebo when he saw me, and I saw him, and we waved. When you don't see your husband for three years, you don't quite know what to expect: greyer hair, a moustache, a pot belly, or increasingly gaunt cheeks. Two out of four.

Coffee is a great mediator. We'd stood in line at the café and I'd watched him order a large dark roast, and held my tongue for the requisite ten seconds before noting, half-jokingly, that he still hadn't managed to quit caffeine though it made him ill. It was a constant struggle, he'd replied. Years earlier, on a street corner in Brighton, a similar remark had resulted in an argument and us taking two separate trains home from our honeymoon.

I stuffed the signed and dated paperwork into a plastic envelope and opened the car door. We were stopped on the side of the road outside the family court, as if we were dropping off a parcel at the post office or popping into the corner shop for a packet of chewing gum. He'd never liked formality much, but I'd learned in the intervening years that a lack of ceremony didn't make things feel any less important. Love, sadness and anger still did their quiet work.

The court was formal and bleak in the way that only buildings related to births, marriages and deaths can be, and a winding staircase tunnelled us down to the basement and the wicket designated for do-it-yourself divorces. Standing in the waiting room, three feet away from another couple retracting their vows, we stood quietly, pretending not to listen.

When we'd finished at the court, we got back into the Toyota and drove to the supermarket. He bought another gallon of Pure Spring Water and loaded it into the back seat. The enormity of the water bottle might have been the last straw for me, if it hadn't already come some years earlier. Standing in the grocery aisle, waiting as he picked over the many varieties of plastic-capped, pasteurised water, I was struck with the feeling, years late, that I no longer had to live like this. I didn't have to wait for some-one else any more. In truth I hadn't lived like this for three years, but that was the first time I'd felt it.

He dropped me off and got out to give me a kiss. A last kiss, perhaps. Maybe we'll see each other again. But, paperwork filed, we could kiss goodbye and mean it. And just as quickly, I got into another car and drove to the ocean. Out of the city, down the coast. And as I swam in the cold of the North Atlantic, it all washed away.

It's late August by now, and I'm beginning to feel the summer slipping away. There's still time, of course, but practicalities are crowding in once more: deadlines, work.

By the end of September, I'm meant to have three chapters of my dissertation ready to submit. I've spent the summer refining them, parsing stories of nineteenth-century social reformers from those of landscape designers, distinguishing the words of Romantic poets from the hours of taped interviews I have with locals from the Heath. As I work my mind is thick and absent, in another land. But when I set out to the lakes, I'm here. My focus will grow sharper as the weather cools. For now, the heat still hangs heavily, but I can see the long stretch of autumn and winter lying ahead of me.

When I'd begun swimming at the beginning of summer, it felt like too great a task, like something onerous I was using to punish myself. *Swim here and swim alone. Make this place yours.* I'd gone into it with anger, with expectation. It was penance. Swim until you find that feeling again, the feeling of freedom. I didn't know that you could love someone and still be free.

Three months on, I've settled into a rhythm. It feels a bit like when you've cycled a long way, your legs in constant rotation, and it's easier to keep moving than to stop. Or when you've stepped off a boat and can still feel the water beneath you, even on dry land. It's becoming normal. It doesn't scare me for now.

I'm on my bike, tracing the route up Prenzlauer Allee. Past the motorway at the edge of the city and on to the long suburban streets that drag through the surrounding villages – all stretched along a single street, bungalow house fronts and shop fronts opening on to the pavement. I bike absent-mindedly, mired in thoughts of upcoming deadlines and a vague concern about having enough water for the day. It's another long trip, and I don't want to repeat that day near Pätz. By now, as my legs have found their rhythm, I've devised a system. I pack a thermos of coffee. A bottle of water. A boiled egg, two slices of bread and a slice of cheese. Two carrots. A piece of chocolate. Every single time. Ritual.

Don't bike so fast. Breathe. Is it time to stop for water? The sun cuts a strong line across the pavement – thirty degrees.

I'm thick in thought when the field opens before me. A scene I've seen a hundred times in a photograph, some photo saved on my phone from that day last November, with Jacob dressed in shorts and a red jacket, leaning on his bike, checking the map. Fields on either side and wind turbines in the distance. To the east, a hillside housing some Soviet bunker or something, he'd said. It was always some Soviet bunker.

I've been here before. Struck by the bizarre recognition of a place I've been to just once but documented and carried around in my pocket for months, I feel strangely at home in the midst of these far-away fields. But glancing to my left, a tiny hunting blind peeks out atop the field. That isn't in my picture. It isn't in my memory of the place. This field, always autumnal in my mind, is now green with late summer and drenched in humid sun. It's bigger than I remember. The reality of the place stretches wider than my memory. I ride on without stopping, a corner of my mind on him.

Ahead I find a village with a crumbling stone church. Curving along the road I reach the point outside the city where the air turns to perfume at Schönwalde, thick with heady green pine and wet fern. Ivy droops from a small thicket of beech trees. My legs begin to tire in the dense, woody humidity. The lake is still ten kilometres away.

At Wandlitz, I duck off the main road and into a quiet lane. It's a town of twenty thousand, taking in the surrounding villages, and I love it. But there are incongruities here. It is a land of lakes, its name literally coming from a Slavic phrase meaning 'people who live by the water'. And so it is: people come here for the water. Politicians from the East. And everyday people, fishermen, swimmers. With Soviet land reform, the lake became the state's, but reunification changed so much. In 2003, a wealthy investor came, and the land beneath the lake was sold. The town couldn't afford to keep it for themselves. Since then – property lines carved up and meticulously attended to – locals have paid rent for access to the lake, though the water is still theirs. Wandlitzer See is a sign of what we stand to lose, a contemporary fable in reunified Germany.

The village road ahead is scattered with families ready for a last summer Sunday, laden with kickboards and kid-sized rubber rings. Crowds huddle in the shade under the bakery's outdoor umbrellas. It isn't even noon yet, but the crowds snake out from the gates of the private *Strandbad*. I'm headed elsewhere.

I duck on to a nearby lane and it's quiet. I lock my bike to a signpost and wander down to the small stretch of green and sand, one of the few access points preserved for the public, abutting the private beach next door. I've hiked around Wandlitzer See a handful of times, but never stopped to swim here. Liepnitzsee is nearby and has become a habit. But now that I've arrived, I wonder if perhaps I've been mistaken to skip it so often.

A deep blue stretches out smoothly towards the horizon, cut only by the occasional swimmer and a cluster of unwittingly humorous stand-up paddle-boarders. I swallow a laugh and take in the small beach, just a thin line of grassy lawn with a sliver of sand edging out into the shallows of the lake. It isn't much.

Undressing and stepping into the cold blue, I find that the shallows extend out a long way. A pair of naked toddlers splash by, and a pair of twenty-somethings in black shorts tap a beach ball between them. Wading out between them, I tuck down and submerge my shoulders in the cold. The lakes have become cooler these past weeks. Autumn is coming.

Swimming out into the bracing wet, I roll on to my back and rest, blue below and blue above, the horizon marked only by swimmers. I could stay here all day, though I know full well that quieter lakes await me. I can't linger if I am going to make it through the day. I have to pack up. A few more minutes in the cold, though, and then perhaps my legs will be ready. The next lake is eight kilometres away.

I plan to go to Großer Lottschesee, a spot of blue I spied on the map a day earlier, having never noticed it before. I'm continually amazed by how they seem to appear, small spots on a digital map I move around with my fingertips. Minuscule ponds and larger stretches of watery promise. My list keeps growing. This one appeared suddenly, as if it hadn't been there before, as I was mapping my route across the northern sections of Wandlitz towards Ruhlsdorf.

But Großer Lottschesee, I find, stands mired behind a

railway line and a strip of fenced-off forest. The small blue line on my map points, instead, to the small, polypous lake to its south, connected by a grassed-in strip of water: Kleiner Lottschesee. A thimble of a lake at the end of a gravelly forest road, edged by a campground and a grassy, tiny park. A lake-side restaurant looms large to its side, and the chatter of older couples hums above the green.

Settling next to a sloping spit of sand between an old man in a lawn chair and a couple watching the shore, I undress quickly and stack my clothes. This will be a quick stop, I decide – it is past noon and I want to eat, but lunch will have to wait until later.

I step quickly into the orange water. Disappearing instantly, my feet feel around instead for some clear ground. Sand, some sharp rocks, but not much else. Feeling safe enough, I push out into the deep, extending my arms ahead of me. It's cold. A crack of fear opens and I think of what's beneath me – opaque orange impeding my vision – and of snakes and sharp-toothed fish and leeches. I want out. I begin to panic, but with a breath, gliding out, I settle my vision on the horizon and focus. *Think only of what you can see.* A fear rebuked, but always returning.

I swim on, out into the middle of the lake and around in an arc, towards another stretch of sandy shore. An old woman slides past me in the water, smiling. She is calm, and all I feel is fear. And then, the shallow returns and I feel my knees bump up against the ground. Back on my feet, I hurry out, my breath heaving after only a few minutes in the water. I hope no one notices.

On the grass again, I wrap my towel around my shoulders and sit down, fumbling through my bag for dry clothes. The old man on the lawn chair, waving off a friend in an accent I've never heard before, turns to me.

'*Ist es kalt?*'

I hesitate and he repeats himself, clarifying.

'*Das Wasser. Das Wetter ist heiß, aber das Wasser ist kalt.*'

I nod, awkwardly fumbling through my explanation that it wasn't too cold, I swim in winter normally, but he's already moved on, registering the ineptitude of my German.

'*Woher kommst du?*'

'*Kanada,*' I reply, receiving a look of confusion. I notice the large hearing aid in his ear and repeat myself, articulating. '*Kanada.*'

'Oh, so you speak English then!' He laughs. 'We all speak English here.'

I apologise. 'I normally try to speak German.' I'm clutching my dry clothes; I need to get going.

'Canada is different,' he begins, and then trails off about his nephew who lives in Quebec but hates it because he moved there from San Diego. 'It's a bit different. Michigan is cold.'

He isn't making sense. I try not to look confused, but I'm struggling to follow his line of thought, nodding. He asks what I am doing here. Explaining briefly how I came to be in Berlin, he registers only that I came via London and laughs in delight.

'So you know all about the English accent then! You lyyyke to swim in layyykes.' He's pleased with himself. Thoroughly confused but smiling, I pack up my things and throw on my clothes. These small fragments, these small exchanges, are a way in to this place. I won't see this man again, and within a few minutes I'll have forgotten this confusing conversation. But it matters to me, all the same.

I pop a handful of almonds into my mouth and stand up, waving goodbye. An awkward exit. He continues laughing to himself. I wish him a good day by the lake and wander off into the woods.

Zum Großer Lottschesee is a small forest lane stretching across the top of the lake. I pedal along it, winding my bike around the steel posts blocking cars from the forest. I'm completely alone.

Eight kilometres along from here sits Bernsteinsee, my third lake of the day, lunch and a rest in the glorious sun. But first this road: closely packed gravel scattered with pine cones, snaking through a pinewood skirted with fern. Sunlight cuts in occasionally, casting bright stripes through the green and orange. There's still the citrus smell of warm pine.

The ground here is bedded moss, and I think of last November again, the moss, the picnic. I'd bring him here, I decide, before remembering that it isn't possible. Even if it was, I wouldn't. I shunt the memory off to the corner of my mind.

Halfway along the lane, the ground softens and the grey gravel becomes sand. My bike shudders and slips in its tracks, and I step off, cursing. I am only halfway there, and if the road is sandy the rest of the way I'll have to walk. It's another four kilometres at least.

Fuck. The trees open into a wide cornfield and what was a sheltered, mild warmth becomes a searing, buzzing heat. A ball of fire in a sky of watery blue. Sand stretches ahead of me, through the fields and past a dilapidated farm building. I have to keep walking.

Thirst creeps to the edges of my mouth. Slinging my back-pack off to get water, I bump my bike bell, and its brisk ring echoes across the land. I am really, really alone out here. Looking down, I notice cloven footprints dotting a winding path on the ground in front of me. There's a hunting blind on the edge of the field, but no one is here.

Twenty minutes pass as I push my bike through the sand. *It's been a lot worse*, I think, all the while cursing the decision to take this road. *Why don't I carry paper maps?* For a moment, I think of that day in Pätz, but then two white posts creep on to the horizon, followed by a cluster of small houses. The end of the road, pavement again. I'm almost there. After that road, the lake.

Through a break in the trees, the turquoise sheet of Bernsteinsee, another former sand quarry, flashes into view. It is said the name emerged because locals used to find bits of amber – fossilised from pine resin – in the lake bed. The reality of it is far less romantic. Children's shrieks hum across the air, and the pavement becomes crowded with beachgoers. I'd never heard of Bernsteinsee until a few weeks ago, but can see immediately that it's not an isolated, secret place. Queues of cars creep into an overflowing car park dropped just beneath an enormous, golden crescent of beach. The sand stretches at least two hundred metres towards the lake, with fringes of grass clumped about, creating nooks along the shore. It is swarming with sunbathers. *This is basically the middle of nowhere*, I think, puzzled, as I lock my lonesome bike amidst the cars.

Torn between principles and hunger, I peek around for an entrance to the lake away from the private *Strandbad*. Private beaches make me furious. But clusters of families line the entrance, and beyond them I see only fences. I'm too hungry for this. I wander towards the gates, ready to pay, but instead see an empty ticket hut. There's no one manning the desk, so I saunter by, glancing to my side in case someone stops me. No one does.

And then the beach opens before me, yellow-gold and dry in all directions, tall grass screening the blue. A line of volleyball nets is busily occupied. A portable DJ stall sends its rhythmic thud into the hot air. This isn't exactly what I'd expected.

I'm desperate to sit down and I search for shade, any-where, but I can't find any. I stumble through the sand towards a quieter corner with a small white sign scrawled in red: *FKK*. *Freikörperkultur,* Germany's naturist move-ment, a remnant of the East, thrives in the lake-going culture. Nearby, a group of older, tanned Germans lie splayed and naked in the sand.

I find a scrap of light shadow beneath a bush and huddle there, my back to the water. Unboxing my lunch, I begin to eat, furiously and with delight. I need to drink water, I remember – it's thirty-two degrees and I've been out for hours. I crack a hard-boiled egg, rolling its crumpling shell along the tupperware's lid. No salt, but it's perfect.

Fed and watered at last, I take in my surroundings. Next to me, a young woman hides in the shade, her red shoul-ders shining. An older couple share a newspaper nearby. I want to sit and rest, but my blanket is stretched atop roots and twigs, so instead I throw off my clothes and tuck them into my back-pack. I wander towards the water through a ten-foot mouth of sand amidst the grass. Old men wade to their knees and children bob with water-wings.

I step in, quickly jog past them, and then the ground drops off suddenly beneath me. *Plötzlich*, the German word for 'suddenly', so perfectly captures the plot-twist motion that finds me swallowing a mouthful of water and searching for my swimming legs, the moment when the foggy shallows turn immediately to deep, mineral green. And suddenly, unexpectedly, I'm afloat.

There is nothing to be afraid of here. Fear forgotten, for now. Jolly swimmers surround me on all sides: a man in cartoonish goggles – *Too old to be in those goggles, like my mother*, I think, *but whatever* – and a greying, round old man, rolling along the water's surface. Ahead of me is a raft, manned by two young boys in trunks and water-wings.

I swim out, looking for stillness, but there's no peace here. The lake itself is a joy – cold and clear – but that summer hum and the distant techno thud carry across the water. I want to be alone. *I want to go again*, I think, restless. I can't sit still today. I have one lake left.

I dodge across the road, and in seconds I'm at Kiessee. The map shows a folded-over rectangle in blue, shaped like a *u*. I see only a large, square building ahead of me, and hear only the mosquito-zip of wires beyond it. I read the sign: *Wasserski*.

Shit. I spent my whole day out and now *this*. Water-skiing? Men in board shorts saunter past while every few moments cheers rise from the crowds. A wakeboarder has splashed some tentative onlookers, who are now laughing in the shallows, soaked. The map said there was swimming here.

I wander past the crush of onlookers, towards a small patch of trees. And then the small cluster of trees opens on to a quiet stretch of lawn and sand, insulated from the zip-line hum of the skiers by a veritable wall of plants. Grass edges along Kiessee's shore, and along the right-hand side of the lake's u-shaped body, I see sloping courses of sand reaching to shore. Like Bernsteinsee across the road, Kiessee is a remnant from the sand pits. A campsite sits along the far edge, but here, there is just a rustic bench and a patch of grass, with still, silent water ahead of me.

Undressing, I peer down into the sandy, pale blue and see a school of striped, glistening perch exploring the shallows. I step in up to my ankles and they remain, scattering only as I walk out up to my waist. The water here is glorious – crisp and glinting, like light filtered through an aquamarine gemstone.

I've been waiting for this lake all summer. Sandy without feeling murky, cold and clear but emerald at its deepest. My toes dance in and out of sight as I tread water, taking in the quietude of this empty lake. The waterskiers have disappeared.

On my back, I trace loops with my legs as I kick out into the centre, pale blue sky gliding above me. Ears underwater, I hear nothing. It isn't a terrifying, muffled nothingness, but a quiet solitude. Stillness, and I float. The nagging November memory leaves me for a moment. I've never been here. This lake is entirely mine. Alone and suspended.

The peace is temporary. Eyes closed, I don't see the grey edging in from the north. But I hear it, a slow rumble, and I know I have to get out. Not for fear of the lake or of the lightning, but because of the rain – I am miles from the nearest train station. I'm at least fifty kilometres into the day and I can't make it all the way home. I need a train and I need to get there before the storm.

Stillness interrupted, I scramble to shore and get dressed into clean clothes: cotton cycling shorts and an old Team GB vest. I'm on my bike within seconds, shunting between parked cars to get back to the main road. I look behind me and see only the slow-motion churn of slate grey. I need to outrun it.

I pass the road sign marking eighteen kilometres to Bernau, where I can catch a train home. But the road is narrow and sloping, a rolling line cut through an enormous tranche of reforested pine. I pedal harder and keep my eyes on the road.

Cars begin to overtake me, and turning over my shoulder my eye is caught by the slightest flash of purple, recognisable to me even at a distance. Heather. I have it tattooed on my side, a single inflorescence etched into my ribcage. I mouth the shape of the word and say it out loud to help me remember. I keep pedalling. Moss is scattered on the hillside.

More cars speed past, and to my right I see only the whisking line of the forest: heather, birch, pine, fern. I repeat them in my head, then with my mouth, cycling in rhythm, and I feel the wind shift. To my right, a field opens and above it looms the dark, inky grey. A line cuts through it like water through pigment, a wet crease to remind me of rain.

I need to bike faster but I come to what I think may be the only hill in Brandenburg. Willing myself up it, I see a crowd of lycra-clad cyclists ahead, giving up and heading for shelter. I follow the road, passing them on the gravel shoulder. In the sudden darkness of another stretch of pines, cars turn their lights on and begin to pass. *It's only four o'clock*, I think, and then realise that the road has darkened to night as the storm rolls overhead. Wind rushes in, and suddenly the air is a mess of pine needles. Warm, fat drops of rain begin to land on my arms. I relent. I need to slow down.

I stop on the roadside to put on my bike lights. Rain now falls heavily in sharp pins and needles, turning the world to a fluid and moving grey. I pedal on as lightning rips into the small crack of sky above the trees.

I'm soaked through, dodging overflowing potholes, when I see it: tucked on to the roadside, a lonesome bus shelter, glass-topped and dry. A black bicycle is lobbed on the road's shoulder, and in the shelter I glimpse the unmissable, cheerful greeting of a flowered summer dress. The woman in it is soaked through too, and she smiles as I dismount and run under the glass roof, laughing uncontrollably.

In the dry of the shelter, we watch sheets of water fall from the sky. The smell of rain washes away the citrus green of pine; everything becomes grey. I check my map and see that I'm still six kilometres from the train in Bernau. Resigning myself to the brief respite, to waiting out the storm, I turn to the woman, who is clutching a blue towel, and ask, '*Hast du geschwommen?*' I have no idea if this is the right verb or conjugation, so I trail off, mumbling. Have you swum?

She laughs and says, yes, before the storm.

In German, I ask her where she has been and she begins to tell me about a nearby lake, just a small one, in the forest. She pulls out a folded paper map, points to a blue spot at its centre, and I look closely. Mechesee.

I've never seen this lake before. Perhaps it isn't on my map, I think momentarily, before regaining good sense and deciding, instead, that some lakes only show themselves when they're ready to. In this moment with a total stranger under a bus shelter in the middle of a forest, in one of the sharpest and briefest storms of summer, I am given a new lake.

south

By September, the heat has lifted. Grey begins to cloud the sky, and sun creeps out only momentarily. Summer leaves as quickly as it arrived. The days pass swiftly as my work grows frantic. Amidst the deadlines, I've taken on part-time work as a nanny. I spend entire days proofreading, linking one sentence to another without coming up for air, and then rush off to meet the kids. I've set out a strict schedule for my work and feel pressure to stick to it. The first chapters of my dissertation are due in a week. But I'm excited. The coming of autumn means cold, and having grown used to the warmth of summer, I'm looking forward to something more. Something bright, and sharp, and different. It starts in the sky. The warmth of the sun disappears first, but soon it'll leave the ground, and then water too.

There's a patch of forest south of Müggelsee, just south of Berlin: young oak and elderberry in alternation, with pine and rowan trees clumped like bristles on the edges.

I've arrived here by bus and a short walk through residential streets. Along the way there's been no one, not even a car. I stop at the forest's edge, unsure, and then follow the dirt track until the late summer sun thins, the thin skeletons of pine growing thicker the farther I walk. Yellow starlets of bird's-foot trefoil break the moss's green, tiny interjections in a silent wood. The wood smoke on the air – a sure sign of summer waning – reminds me that I'm not far out, just at the edge of the suburbs, though I'm alone amidst the trees. A kilometre into the woods, I find an errant patch of mint, grown thick in the absence of anyone else, and I wonder how it got here.

Then there's the lake, Krumme Lake, so close in name to my first Berlin lake, Krumme Lanke. I'll find these Slavic-named 'crooked lakes' across Brandenburg, like a connect-the-dots puzzle that's secret and special only to me. Between here and the thin rivulet veins of the Müggelspree lies a bog, newly restored and thick with grass and sphagnum.

Luca, the brazen Italian I've been renting my studio space from, had told me about this lake, a crooked, lily-capped stretch of water at the end of the watershed. He'd promised to come. But it's September now, and he's declared swimming season over. Weeks earlier, his incredulity at the idea of swimming through winter felt like a challenge, and now, on my own, I have something to prove.

I've come alone, and though I'm grateful for the peace of the forest, when I reach the lake I feel a ripple of fear. It hasn't been strong this summer but the changing season seems to sharpen my fear. The rising heat of panic as I step near the water's edge. I've been walking for an hour alone and I realise, stepping in to the water, how far I am from anyone else. Why hadn't there been anyone else on the path? I'd wanted the solitude, I tell myself, inching knee-deep into the lake. But something isn't right: it's too beautiful, too quiet. It can't be safe. My legs ache to get out. My pulse moves to my eardrums, and I retreat to shore.

I can't *not* swim. I'm immediately ashamed, swearing quietly into the silence. A patch of sunlight moves across the rippled lake surface and I decide to take the opportunity, ploughing back into the water, waist-deep, the roar of water breaking the air. I'm in and swimming, still panicking but afloat, and I begin to count my strokes. The winter swimmer's negotiation: stroke-counting, the thing to get you in the water and the thing that keeps you safe. I count to forty-five and I'm out again, still angry with myself. Forty-five is what I'll swim in winter, when there's ice. Here there's a slice of warm sun and a lake full of blossom, and it's *September*. I have to get back in, and I do, but it's a stubborn dance, forcing my legs into the water when something small, old, and unused at the very bottom of my skull is saying to get out. This can't happen now.

After the houseboating trip to Lake Temagami when I was eight, I didn't go near another lake for years. It didn't matter much: I didn't feel especially Canadian at that point. My parents were busy wrangling with their newfound success in business, the new worlds opened to them and their kids through their good fortune and hard work. We didn't spend our holidays by the lakes, unlike many other Canadians, and if I wanted to swim there was always the safety of the swimming pool. After their divorce, I kept up swimming at the YMCA. I'd joined the school swim team, and between training and lessons, I was swimming four times a week. My hair smelled of chlorine, and I grew to love it. The fact of my being a strong, regular swimmer seemed only to underscore the absurdity of lakes, of stepping into deep water when perfectly good pools lay in wait. Pools were safe, sterile, domesticated. In lakes, there seemed to be a wildness and danger I couldn't comprehend.

This is what I struggle to make sense of now: I was a great swimmer. I'd been in lessons for years, earning embroidered badge after badge, until, by sixteen, I was diving to the bottom of the deep, retractable-bottomed pool to retrieve weighted bricks. Even *that* pool stopped scaring me.

But in front of a lake, I fell apart. There was no amount of skill and training that could intervene, no sensible way to reason with it. In front of a lake, I felt fear clearly, purely. It wasn't negotiable.

This is how it would go. Someone, usually my father, would tell me to get in the water. I'd just stand there, staring. The hollow, dark feeling would spread across my chest, and I'd keep staring at the water. The longer I stared, the worse it got. The feeling would spread downwards, into my legs, and then upwards across my shoulders, into my skull. There would be sound: that electric, hazy humming that comes when you've stood up too quickly or smacked your head hard against something. It would surround everything, until I could no longer hear my father encouraging me into the water. And then, in a sheet of dark red, vision would go.

By that point, it was too late. There was no getting into the water. My only chance was in that small moment between sensing, thinking, and feeling. Before I could register what was happening. This wasn't about over-coming fear, but about getting there *first*, beating it to the punch. Wedging something into that tiny space between the lake and my terror. I was never fast enough.

I haven't seen Sam since New Year's Day, when we'd broken through the ice in Krumme Lanke. The winter swimmers I know in Berlin can be counted on one hand, but he's one of them. I hope he'll be an ally in the coming weeks, someone to keep me company. With someone else around, my fear feels less solid. It turns to vapour, and I can swim through it. By now, the summer has dissolved into autumn, and in the mornings a damp mist rises from the ground.

The broad avenue of plane trees that cuts through the middle of Treptower Park is one of my favourite sights in autumn, but I know it is thinner now than it was just a few years ago. These trees and many others are being lost to Massaria fungus, changing this sheltered stretch of road dramatically. Even so, they are bright in the autumn sky, green turning to orange in the cool air.

This is one of the few swims I'll take within the borders of Berlin. Within the city history arrives more thickly than in the country, the stories more present. Stone and con-crete hold the past in this way, I think. Open and abrupt. In the countryside, it grows over with green and settles into the landscape. The city stone is a monument. The park is a record, one of Berlin's earliest municipal parks. In the final days of the Second World War, it became hard-fought-for territory between the Soviets and Germans.

The Soviet War Memorial occupies the centre of Treptower Park, enormous but stark, a graveyard for fallen soldiers. We cycle around it, racing our bikes towards Karpfenteich – 'Carp Pond' – the hooked stretch of water in the middle of the park. Excavated in the 1880s, the pond sits amidst orderly paths, a swathe of reflective, autumn colour amidst the nineteenth-century park ideal. Swimming here is like swimming in a painting, bright and still.

Leaning our bikes against the trees, we undress and step into the water. The mildewy smell of leaves rises up as our feet sink into the muck, but the water is clear enough, so we swim out into the cold. It's blue in the sky and brown in the water. We swim towards the horizon: a riot of colour in the turning trees. The water will turn soon too.

autumn

Overturn: The top of the lake cools and sinks to the bottom. As the season changes, wind mixes the lake until it settles.

a pool of light

It's the end of September, but a day so bright arrives that I have to swim. I want a journey. A day of solitude to make sense of my own feelings at the shift of the seasons and the completion of an enormous part of my work. The summer had been so bright and so busy that I'd become caught up with deadlines and hooked into the trace of adrenaline that comes with long days out on the bike and at the lakes. Reaching the lakes had become a task, and the rhythm I'd found worked especially well in the warm weather, when I could be out for hours with the summer light stretching before me. But the reality of my decision, by autumn, is beginning to settle on me.

Half the year, Berlin is a dark place. Not the permanent night of the north, but a slowly settling grey. By mid-autumn, when the time changes, the sun will be down by four, and in mid-winter, by three-thirty. Sunken low into the ground, so much of the city seems dark even in daylight. In the past weeks I've found myself mostly alone and often tired. As if when the heat lifted and the cool settled, something settled in me, too, and it is taking all of me to wrestle it back into the world. It isn't depression – I know that too, and this isn't it – but sadness. The kind of mourning that accompanies the change in the seasons, and the realisation that time is passing and I'm still here, doing this thing. Homesickness – for friends, for familiar places – comes in thick waves, turning solitude to isolation. With summer I'd found a rhythm in carrying out my swims, in visiting these places, but the core of it was something I'd been avoiding. It appeared that day at Krumme Lake, when I'd been scared to swim. This small fragment of loneliness and fear. In autumn, I know, I'll have to make peace with it.

I take the train to Spandau, just west of the old 1930s Olympic Stadium, and bike the rest of the way to Sacrower See. The ride is easy, down a suburban road that at one point could be anywhere in my childhood. An Esso station at one corner, a KFC on the other. It's as if we already know these places, wherever they appear. Comfort and heartbreak wrestled into commercial premises.

Beyond the sprawl, fields and trees emerge, punctuated only by the occasional village. Eventually the quiet road turns into a gravel path, and then into forest. The quiet comes slowly too, and by the time I reach the forest my mental chatter has slowed to a silent halt. I've been working all hours this week, writing towards a deadline, and desperately need this swim to set me right. I've come here searching.

This forest, the lake and the quiet roads that run through here sit uneasily at the city's edge, indifferently tucked alongside the Havel River. I wheel my bike into the woods and along the road to where signs mark the border that used to be here, and as I'm wandering the trees I realise that this trail is part of the Berliner Mauerweg, the path marking the Cold War border. The trail was established between 2002 and 2006, one of the ways the city and local campaigners have sought to make use of remnant land in the footprint of the Wall. Birch wood creeps on to the roads, reclaiming the ground. It is hushed and sheathed in the most distant kind of sadness – like so much of the city – but breaks in the trees are interrupted by the brightest of blues. The water sits in the distance.

As I push my bicycle along the sandy trail a father and son bike past, stopping briefly to ask me about my bike. I chat to the father for a while, and then realise I'm speaking about my bike as I would speak of a friend. *She* is fantastic, I say, so reliable. Wishing me a good day, they bike off ahead, enjoying their Sunday. There is something in the simplicity of their manner, quietly biking side by side, that moves me. I hold my bicycle close to my side, the dark green frame aglow with the pine, and as they disappear around a bend I duck off the trail to find a place to swim.

There's an alder tree shading a tiny, sandy cove on the lake, so I settle and step into the diaphanous wet. The water has a cut-glass clarity, the kind that regular swimmers say is noticeable just as the water begins to turn with the season. You only notice it if you swim often enough to know the water, to recognise the moment when the suspended residue of summer settles and the clearest water is left at the surface. It doesn't stay this way, but for a few magical moments in autumn the water is crystalline, like swimming through a gemstone.

The dregs of summer warmth have quickly disappeared and the water is cool at the surface, so I swim out into the sun and paddle backstroke in circles until I'm tired. There's no one here, and for the first time in a while I feel completely at ease, without a glint of fear. My breath stops short as I think that this place has always been here, at this border place. Sacrower See was in the East, right near the Wall. Who swam here then?

I swim to shore and dry off, then walk farther along the forest path that brushes the eastern edge of the lake. A short way in, I find another clearing with a much larger, sunnier beach, and there sit the father and son, now reading comics to one another in the afternoon warmth. I smile and set my bike against a tree, getting ready to swim again. Something about this end of the lake feels different, more open and warmer, so I paddle out and lie in the sun a while, until cloud creeps in and I begin to feel cold. It's almost October.

Warmly dressed again, I bid the father and son good-bye and set off out of the forest. There's a short-cut out of the woods so I won't have to loop back. I wheel my bike towards the trail's end, nodding at the passing Sunday strollers who meet me along the way. It's a busy afternoon on the trail, but something in the swim shifted me and I'm grateful for my own solitude.

Near the edge of the wood, I'm struck by a tiny flash of pale pink in the green. Terrestrial orchids, I think at first, but I look closer and see that it's a patch of Himalayan balsam, an invasive snapdragon. They are aliens here. In other parts of Germany, they're encouraging people to eat their stems in order to eradicate them. Its thin, toothed-leaved stalks can grow metres tall, shading out other plants, and its seeds erupt and spread when disturbed. But this one is small. The floral pink in September is striking, so I stop to look at the labial flowers. Few plants attract such hatred, but I can't help but find them beautiful. I stoop down low to look at them.

I'm ignoring the flies buzzing at my feet. Satisfied with the balsam, I step back, but the insect hum grows louder. As I look down I realise the ground beneath me is dried a deep red. It's blood, and there are flies everywhere.

I glance along the trail, but there's no one else here now. I can't see where the sound is coming from, but I can hear flies, loads of them. Though I should probably keep moving – I can see the road from here – I'm frozen in place, craning my neck to see the source of the insect radio fuzz. It's in the bushes. Someone has moved whatever died here off the path, and in a horrifying haze I'm walking towards it, picking through the scrub.

A pile of red organs sit to one side, and next to it, some unidentifiable thing, skin picked clean, covered in the blue-black of flies. A deer, perhaps, or a dog. I look closely but can't recognise it, and as I stare the numbness dissipates and I feel only a churning sickness in my stomach. It rises, so I turn and walk, pushing my bike as far out of the woods as I can, as quickly as I can, trying not to be sick. I'm on the road again before I regain my senses, and ride back into town with a knot of disgust and fear in my gut, wondering if the clarity I'd found in the middle of the lake could only ever be temporary.

*

Later that night I awake from sleep and, wrapped in a coat and scarf, wander into the middle of Volkspark Friedrichshain. No one else is out, so I stand alone in the middle of a clearing edged only by a thin larch tree. I stand, eyes to the sky, watching as the incandescent white moon is swallowed, inch by inch, by a dark red, coppery and cold. It's a rare combination of a super moon, as the moon reaches its fullest point nearest to earth, and a lunar eclipse. The blood moon is the first in my lifetime.

I wait in the clearing for an hour, half-awake, watching the white turn to red, until the last remnants of light shine their brightest crescent. In this light, the usually flat disc of the moon takes its full shape, spherical and more real than I've ever seen, like a cold rock given life. Blood red in the night.

Fully eclipsed, I watch it a while, my heart swelling in the darkness, before making my way back to home, back to bed. Outside my apartment, a father and son are stood looking at the sky, wrapped in blankets, eyes pinned to the eclipse. And I remember that this won't happen again for a long time; this will be the only time this father can take his young son out to see the blood moon. I think of the other father and son, out at the lake, basking in the September sun, reading aloud. For a moment I feel at home again in this place in the middle of the city. The day that has passed no longer feels so dire, and I sleep knowing the sky glows red in the dark.

a congregation

It's the first weekend in October, and I've set out for what might be my last long day trip before winter. I'm travelling much farther than usual, drawn to the magic of a lake I've only ever read about. Out the train window lie fields ploughed green and brown like corduroy, a patchwork of fields sewn together by irrigation ditches. Between two of them, a dump site is piled with soil and refuse, and amidst the piles is a cluster of sunflowers, tangled together as if in embrace. It's a moment of tenderness amidst a strewn-about sadness, like the flowers had taken the time to bring sentiment to a discarded place.

I spend the swift train journey to the northern end of the state staring out of the window. I've managed to hold on to the stillness of last week, the ease I found in solitude. I've longed for today. This one day in the week when I set out on my own, the lake at its end, blue and cool, salvation. I hope. As we approach Gransee, the train slows and I catch sight of three skydivers falling in disarray on the wind, faster than the train, like bats in the night. They fall like scattered seeds, and then catch the air and are pulled out of sight. The train is arriving.

I lug my bike on to the platform and check the map. I've come prepared for a long day – the hour-long train journey to be followed by an hour on the bike, before I reach the woods and need to walk. I've made an exception in coming here: Großer Stechlinsee sits at the farthest northern edge of Brandenburg, a far cry from the other lakes I've swum this year. Earlier in the week I'd met with Michael, a freshwater ecologist, and he'd said I must visit.

The Rheinsberg Nuclear Power Plant sits nearby, slowly undergoing the process of decommissioning since German reunification. Once a prized demonstration of East German technology, the plant has sat disused since 1990. As one of the first nuclear power plants in Germany – and the first to be decommissioned – it is a stark interruption in what has become a quiet landscape. As dismantling has carried on, the plant and its machinery have sat like a time capsule in the forest: yellowing panels with buttons and dials, ageing control rooms that look like cut-outs from mid-century design magazines. Still, workers populate its hallways, quietly winding up their work.

Before 1990, the water that cooled its reactors poured out into Stechlinsee, heating the lake. Now, the lake's crisp, almost neon blue-green sits quietly, a still life in an empty sky. Stirring the foam of his coffee, Michael had spoken of the water's clarity and assured me of its safety. The record, he'd said, is in the sediment, as heavy metal contamination from the plant settles into the upper layers of ground sediment in the lake.

Ten minutes from the station, I'm cycling a paved forest path. The wind has picked up, and as I cycle my mind is on the skydivers I'd seen from the train. Their haphazard fall, the trust it must take, like being caught in a current. When you get pulled out by a rip current, you're meant to swim sideways, parallel to the shore, to choose right or left. You aren't supposed to struggle. But falling through the air, you don't get a choice.

I'm cycling absent-mindedly, not really here at all, and then – *thwack* – I'm called back. An acorn dances off the top of my brow, narrowly missing my eye, a tiny force that nearly topples me. *Be here*, it seems to say. I reach up and check my stinging brow: no blood. I pay attention. The forest around me is a thin stand of oak, swathed in orange. I want to be here, in autumn, at the far end of the state, so far from the city, moving through the wood.

The trail opens on to a quiet residential street, and I'm reminded of the thinly populated landscape of Fontane's *Der Stechlin*, the novel that brought this lake into Germany's popular imagination. His name still carries weight here: a species of whitefish that occurs only here bears his name, Fontane's cisco. Scientists are trying to determine how the fish came to be here – and only here – in this isolated place.

Fontane's literary Stechlinsee has a plate-glass stillness, no birds or boats, and springs to life only in moments. He describes the Legend of the Red Rooster, in which Stechlin erupted with geysers in tandem with far-off seismological events, like the Lisbon earthquake of 1755. As the geysers broke the surface of the water, a red rooster was seen flapping its wings angrily, whipping the lake into waves. The myth has preoccupied not just Fontane, but scientists too. At one time, seismologists sought to study the lake and its legend. Even today, in one study of the lake's algae, scientists surmised that the 'Red Rooster' may simply have been an accumulation of *Planktothrix rubescens*, a red-hued algae. Now, a painting of a rooster adorns the walls of the Leibniz-Institute for Freshwater Ecology and Inland Fisheries, which has a laboratory on Stechlin.

Today, I find the lake calm. The forest surrounding the lake isn't the orderly, patient timber-wood of Brandenburg's silviculture industry. It's all sloping hillsides and mosses, diverse and alive. I lead my bike off the road and into the trees, the sheen of water on the horizon, wheeling into the silence. My bike cracks over a branch, and I look up, terrified, the sound breaking the stillness. Ahead of me on the path a pair of eyes stare back, ten pairs actually, antlered, locking my gaze with theirs, and then they dodge off, all legs, into the pine. There must be hunting blinds nearby.

I come to a footbridge, and from here can see out over the whole of the lake, flat and cool. Looking down, I can see right to the bottom, the crooked clumps of molluscs dotting the sandy floor. Sound seems to have vacated this place, as if I were standing at the centre of an empty cathedral, a hollow stone cavern, but the sun moves over me and I remember that I'm outside. A voice echoes out over the water from maybe a mile away and makes the place seem emptier than it is. Fontane wrote that in this part of the country a kind of unconditional silence reigns.

Off the bridge, I stop amidst a cluster of beech trees, crouch low to the ground, and count mushrooms. I've never seen so many in one place, certainly not around Berlin, where the hollow monotony of pine is a constant companion. But here there are at least twenty, a record of a landscape left untouched by tree-felling, a forest in its full diversity. Fly agarics in reds and yellows, stiff polypores, the shiny white caps of a mushroom I've never seen before. I can't keep track and I begin to grow dizzy, so stop at a rough-hewn bench and prepare to swim.

While the air is cooling, the water isn't too cold yet. I slip in, taking tentative steps out into the sand, my feet prickling on the shells. The sky is completely still, but I can still hear the echo of voices somewhere else on the trail, and somehow it leaves me feeling more alone. It is vast, and I'm afraid. I think of the power plant, and the gap of fear opens wider in me. But looking out over the flat of the lake, I'm reminded that it's beautiful too – it can be both – so I swim out, the clear water dipping deep beneath my kicking legs. I'm a dark and moving figure at the water's surface.

The Leibniz-Institute of Freshwater Ecology and Inland Fisheries sits on the eastern shore of Stechlin. Germany is awash with research institutes like this one – indeed, I first came to Berlin because of one – due to a relative glut in funding for independent research across the sciences and humanities. The Institute has laboratories on both Stechlinsee and Müggelsee, enabling scientists to compare the dramatic depth of the former with the shallow enormity of the latter.

Here, the Institute maintains a floating lake laboratory, a series of twenty-four 'mesocosms', shaft-like tubes that extend all the way to the lake's bottom. It is among the most advanced laboratories of its kind. The mesocosms, which are about the volume of a small pond, enable scientists to study the lake in miniature. As the lab remains in place all year, the Institute is able to run experiments in every season, as the lake undergoes its transformation from the sunwashed clarity of summer to the frozen immensity of winter.

I've been reading scientific articles about Stechlinsee, looking up new terminology in *The Treatise on Limnology*, in textbooks and online, trying to understand what makes Stechlinsee so remarkable. I'm beginning to sense the differences between the lakes I've visited, the ways their annual cycles differ from one another. In temperate, deep lakes like Stechlinsee, the layers of the water stratify according to changes in temperature. Lakes like Stechlinsee are known as dimictic: deep lakes that mix fully twice a year, with spring and autumn overturn. In winter, they are covered with ice. The movements of the water – lake stratification and overturn, the lake's turning – are the cycles that keep the lake alive, ever-changing, breathing oxygen into every part of the lake.

Water is at its densest at four degrees celsius. In spring, the surface of the water warms beyond this limit and circulates, mixing the entire lake from top to bottom. As the water warms, it creates a layer of water known as the epilimnion. The deeper you go, the colder it gets. The epilimnion then sits atop a denser, colder layer called the hypolimnion. If you've ever felt the cold of the lake with the tips of your toes treading water in summer, you'll have a sense of how dramatically temperature changes with depth.

By early summer, the epilimnion will have grown thicker as the world around it has transformed with the season. Between the epilimnion and the hypolimnion, the thermocline will have emerged: a mixed, unstable layer of water, the transitional zone of the lake. Unable to mix with the colder, denser water below, the waters at the lake's surface circulate only within themselves, providing an ideal, warm environment for algae to bloom. It is in this summer stagnation that the lake faces the possibility of *umkippen* – when algae thrives in the epilimnion and starves the lake of light, leading plants to decompose and consume the lake's oxygen. The lake can turn a stagnant green. It's why, by September, swimming can seem so unattractive.

But the autumn cold arrives, and wind mixes the lake again. The warmth at the surface decreases until it can no longer remain stratified from the colder water below. As the waters mix again, the lake undergoes autumn overturn.

When the ice comes in winter, the lake faces another period of stratification. The temperature drops. Most of the lake sits around four degrees. At the very surface, just below the ice, the lake is at its coldest. Here, below the ice, the water is at its lightest. The sheet of ice floats on the lake's coldest point, the thin realm between the ice and the depths of the lake. But this entire process is a matter of circumstance: as the climate changes, scientists worry for these winter lakes. As our winters warm, by the end of the century, the ice may not appear at all.

It's luminous, thin, the clearest water I've ever seen. A tree has fallen on the lake's edge and is alive with algae, brighter than green. The algae here get a lot of light – the clarity of the water assures it – and the green glow that blankets the tree's branches underwater is a testament to it. It may be a species of *Cladophora*, which spreads its thick green filaments across fallen trees in fresh water, as well as a number of species of diatoms, unicellular green algae that thrive in Stechlin. Nearly a decade ago, scientists were raising alarms about the quality of the lake, worried that the species diversity in the nutrient-poor water was falling starkly. *Cladophora* algae were one of the few things thriving and were a sign of the level of disturbance in the lake. Algae can be a barometer.

As the climate changes, the much maligned blue-green algae, *Cyanobacteria*, are also set to thrive. With too many nutrients, *Cyanobacteria*, along with other species, can bloom and saturate a body of fresh water, depriving it of oxygen as it decomposes, leading to wider problems like fish death. This is part of the process of *umkippen*, one of the many ways in which algae and bacteria can indicate the health of a lake. But today, the clarity of the water and the brightness of this small bloom of green are a joy to behold. It is not the choking stuff of a stagnant lake, but alive and clear. In the water, it seems aglow.

I swim to shore, the cold slipping off my skin, and clamber back to the bench. In the air again, my wet skin cleaves tightly to my body and I shiver. Goosebumps appear across my arms, so I dress quickly, wiping the strange water from my limbs. I too feel aglow – warmth and cold rushing over my skin in tandem. This feeling will be my companion in the coming months.

I eat my lunch on the bench, watching the mirror glass

of the lake. Nothing moves. But sound continues to break the silence, echoing out over the glass as over a canyon. My fear has lifted. The quiet here isn't an emptiness. Rather, it's as if the forest is holding something bright and alive, and holding it very still. I wonder if I'm intruding in this place.

I walk the forest for what feels like hours, following the trail around the lake's edge, and then back through the woods. And then, afternoon waning, I step back on to my bike and pedal along the concrete paved road out of the trees. Just ahead of me, a flash of orange appears on the road, motionless and waiting. A fox. I keep pedalling, a movement that feels like stillness, and make eye contact. We stare as the distance between us recedes. And then the fox turns – its full, copper tail cutting the air – and runs alongside me. We run in the same direction, moving in time. But the road to town is opening ahead of me. The fox steps off the pavement and into the forest, into the deep orange of the pine, and is gone.

small intimacies

I've become accustomed to solitude. The quiet swell of warmth that I know as kindness has settled on me in these moments alone. At Krumme Lake, when my terror returned, there had been a moment when all I could feel for myself was anger. Anger and shame and hatred, hot in my heart, a sharp point in between my ribcage. I was pathetic, a failure, and would never manage this stupid task. I spoke to myself pointedly, admonishingly, cruelly.

As a child, when I would scrape a knee or bump my head, my mother would cradle me close and repeat, gently, 'Be brave, *Baobai*, be brave.' She has called me 'baby' in Chinese my whole life. I was the youngest. She calls my nephew *Baobai* now, and when she says it, we both look up.

My mother gently asked me to be brave and held me securely. Hers was not the voice in my head. Mine was angry, punishing, violent. I'd forced myself back into the lake that day, and I'd hated every moment of it.

Now, it feels strange to feel warmly about being with

myself. The window of anger that had opened at Krumme Lake closed quickly – though it was there – and I'd found a comfort in solitude, in riding my bike across the flat Brandenburg countryside, cold wind whipping my hair and rushing into my ears. I'd found that place in the lake, and in the forest, a kind of stillness in motion.

Today, though, I'm not alone. Coco is here, her red flash of hair dancing at the corner of my sight-line as we walk side by side. We're planning our escape as we walk, deciding what essentials we would want to have ready for the end of the world. Having graduated into the recession and spent the past years wondering what this precarious world might hold, calamity is always at the tips of our tongues. Coco is one of the only people I can imagine fleeing with. Her company, I think, is not unlike solitude, comforting and steady. This thought sends glimmers of warmth through my body.

Groß Köris sits fifty kilometres south of the city, and from here we're walking north-east, along cobbled village streets and on to a thinly forested trail. Fontane travelled here in the final volume of his *Rambles*, travelling by boat and coach around the region between the Oberspreewald, in Brandenburg's south-east, and the Dahme River. It was sparser, then, but remains much the same. Fontane recounts visits to quiet villages lined with orchard trees and expanses of heath and woodland. It is Brandenburg as I've come to know it.

Today, the trail we are walking is lined with fly agaric, some insect-eaten and drying in the cool sun. We crouch down low and press at them with sticks, tracing their crooked lines for yards along the trail. Standing up, we find ourselves at an abandoned, crumbling cabin. The roof has fallen inwards, and as we pick our way through the rubble we see that the living room is still furnished. Water-stained 1970s floral wallpaper still lines the walls. Behind the cabin, we find a blue bicycle, intact but for a missing wheel, its frame bent slightly out of shape, rusting into the ground. Everything is here, an entire life caved in on itself and open to the elements. It's been here a while and leaves me suddenly, fleetingly sad.

We make our way back on to the trail and keep walking. We're planning to loop Klein Köriser See today, following the fourteen-kilometre *Rundweg* that leads us around the lake. The trail isn't isolated, but it's well enough into autumn that the lake is quiet. A quarter of the way around, we stop for lunch and a swim.

Coco hasn't swum since summer, so my assurance that the water isn't all that cold doesn't get her far. She steps in and gasps, immediately retreating to shore, while I swim out into the lake's sunny centre. The lake is strewn with leaves, and as I dry off back on shore I realise that the truest cold will be coming soon.

After swimming, we stroll slowly through the woods, eventually rounding the lake's southern shore near the village of Klein Köris. Along the village road, there stands an oak tree elaborately carved into a three-headed dragon. It catches our attention because there's little else nearby: some boat rentals, houses and a busy road. The *Drachenbaum*, 'Dragon Tree', stands at the edge of the road, watching the traffic.

The tree's nearness to the road contributed to its demise: when it began to rot in the late 1990s, local officials deemed the tree unsafe for traffic, but to fell it would have been devastating. In 1871, at the end of the Franco-Prussian War, the people of Klein Köris had planted the oak as one of two 'peace trees' in the town. The tree's story is displayed on a placard, and reads like a eulogy to village life.

The reason for two peace trees was down to local conflict: no one could agree on where to plant the tree, so two trees were planted, and this particular oak by the lake happened to thrive. The threat of felling emerged over a century later. The decision to save the oak's trunk by carving it into a dragon – an effort led by local dragon boaters – spoke of small-town solidarity about a hundred years late.

Coco and I peer at the tree and the story on the placard, but the afternoon warmth is growing thin and we need to get back. The train is due soon, and we have plans back in the city. As we walk on, though, I turn to glance at the tree, which stands bulkily and clumsily by the road, and I think about the small intimacies of Brandenburg, and how I'll never get to know them all.

At eighteen, I'd devised my escape plan. I'd grown studious and serious the previous year, knowing it would provide a way out of the complications of family life and the small city I'd grown up in. I had the naive idea that a change of surroundings would enable a total transformation: that I might distance myself from the anger I felt at home, and from the fear that I too would slip into emotional precariousness. I could shroud myself in education, could outsmart depression and instability. If I could be intelligent, then I would be good, and then everything would be okay. I'd been accepted into university two thousand kilometres from home. I wanted nothing more than to leave.

There was a city on the east coast that could be mine. A quadrangle of college buildings filled with books I could read, and all of this would be my salvation. Naturally, I had a boyfriend there, waiting for me to move to Halifax to join him.

I had grown up with so many privileges, but the world of books and culture and ideas wasn't among them. I overcompensated: I studied too hard, typed up my hand-written notes every day at the end of class, sat in the front row, answered every question. I did well, academically speaking.

But my personal life was a mess. Despite the physical distance from home, the inconstancy of my previous life seemed to trail behind me, and there was no space between myself and my overblown reactions. I had never witnessed another option and clung desperately to what I believed were solutions. Work, love. The emotions and reactions most people would have relegated to their diaries, I enacted out loud, in public. My boyfriend and I broke up and reconciled weekly. I sat on the stairs of my dormitory crying, begging for acquaintances to console me. Afterwards, I would throw myself all the harder into work, believing it would change me. I got a part-time job as a nanny, then another in a café. I joined the campus newspaper. I swore and raged and threw furniture at home. I grew busier and tenser than ever, swinging violently between two options. Work or fall apart.

I carried on this way for two years. By the summer after the second year, the detritus of overwork, exhaustion, my rages and my desperate need for succour were beginning to swallow me. My boyfriend – to this day, one of the kindest men I've known – broke up with me at last. I don't blame him. I had it coming. Afterwards, I fell apart.

The Nova Scotian summer was turbulent. The weather swelled from damp winter to an almost blue warmth, and then it rained and rained. The grey spread over everything – fog clouded the morning and rain soaked the night. The air had the petrichor scent of salt and worms, the smells of the harbour and dirt after the rain.

I started walking at night, headphones on, listening to a song called 'The Hypnotist's Son' on repeat. I thought the song felt like the hollow in the middle of my chest, the churning pit of my stomach. The song talked about being swallowed by love, about being swept out to sea by it. I had only ever felt love as this gravitational pull, this force that left me unmoored. I had never learned to anchor myself, and all the schoolwork and part-time jobs in the world wouldn't solve it. The nights would pour with warm rain, and I would walk and cry and listen to the song, tracing rectangles through the streets between campus and my apartment.

At home in my apartment, I drank beer and coffee in alternation. My roommate had left a bottle of amaretto on the kitchen counter, and I drank that too. I rolled and smoked joints in bed and left them half-crumpled in an ashtray on my window-sill. I sought the vacancy of drink or drug, but retreated terrified from its edge. I turned to sex, to passing comfort.

One night, I sat in the dark smoking after a doleful one-night stand with a friend of a friend. He awoke and asked me what was wrong, and all I did was shrug. I wanted the feeling of this other person's body off my skin. The next day I slept with my ex-boyfriend, one last time, as if it might fix how I felt.

Two weeks later, when my period didn't arrive, I took the tests, went to the doctor, stopped drinking and smoking. I kept crying. My ex-boyfriend came with me to the hospital, navigated the maze of locked doors, internal stairways and elevators that led to the windowless clinic. He held my hand in the pink waiting room, where re-runs of *Saved By The Bell* played on repeat.

The gel felt cold on my stomach. I watched the ultrasound pulsing on the screen. And then I scheduled an abortion.

I think about that screen sometimes, about the bean-shaped glow at its centre, and calculate the years that have passed. What would my life have looked like?

I kept up my night walking. I resumed drinking and smoking, heartbroken by what sex had brought, and began wandering tipsy past the Armdale Rotary towards Chocolate Lake. It sat just on the edge of the city, so named because a chocolate factory had once sat on the site. A quarry had been dug and left behind this barren, sterile lake. I'd never truly swum in a lake, but there, it no longer scared me.

I stripped out of my clothes in the dark. There weren't street lights, just the big mouth of the moon agape in the sky. I started to swim. Out into the cold, into the dark, into the lake.

*

It's late October, and there is frost on the air. I've been nursing a cold and feel warm with fever, but am restless as ever. I decide that I need a swim. Just walking to the end of my street fills my legs with heavy exhaustion, but a cracked-open, cavernous feeling has been washing over my chest as I've stayed home, and I don't want to feel it. I text Sam and ask if he'll join me.

I lug my bike up the stairs at Karow Bahnhof, ten minutes before the train arrives. I feel faint. Once Sam arrives, though, I immediately feel better: other people do that to me, their presence like an anaesthetic. Sweat stops beading on my forehead, and I regain command of legs.

We take the train as far as Basdorf, a village twenty-five kilometres north of the city, and from here we cycle north, through Wandlitz and on towards Bogensee. After Wandlitz, the road is freshly tarmacked and cuts a narrow strip between symmetrical rows of pine. The monotony of pine is broken by the occasional grove of beech trees. Sam stops near one and touches the bark, talking about beech trees from his childhood back in England. I'm only half-listening. Instead I'm watching his hand on the smooth width of the tree, imagining the sensation of the bark. We cycle on.

Just before the road curves south again, we duck off on to a forest road, winding through the pines and into a small valley of beeches. Past here, we churn our bikes up a small hill until we've reached Bogensee. An ageing, peeling placard shows the map and marks out where we are. It's just an empty stretch of road.

On one side of the road, there's a forestry school; we can hear the distant hum of a chainsaw. Beyond the bushes on our left, there's an enormous, crumbling complex of looming Soviet-era architecture, rows of windows revealing a decaying, lavish interior. It was once a high school for the Free German Youth (FDJ) in the East, a kind of scout or guide movement. The buildings now stand empty, with no hope of a buyer. It's sprawling and enormous, grown over with bramble. Once in a while, the sound of an attendant's weed-strimmer rips into the silence. The local government is hoping to keep it from total disrepair.

We pass the buildings and round the corner, coming to a much smaller, more modest villa. Its roof slopes low to the ground, such that the whole house seems to be working its way into the soil, not so much rotting as sinking under its own weight. In its small courtyard stands a sculpture of a couple embracing. They are rigid, holding one another both close and far apart, their intimacy uncomfortable. I circle them, feeling their stony distance.

Joseph Goebbels – the chief Nazi propagandist – lived here. It is said he brought women here for sex, hiding his affairs in the countryside. He wrote propaganda here. Brandenburg has been trying to sell the property for years; they're careful about whom they sell it to, though, wary of neo-Nazis, and they have yet to find a buyer who passes muster. The house is beautiful, but discomfort seeps into the ground around it.

Sam and I pick our way across the property, peering into the windows. It's immaculate inside. The parquet looks warm in the autumn sunlight. Curtains line the window-frames. The doors are all locked; it's well-kept, but desolate.

This desolation is catching, so we lock our bikes and wander down into the forest, away from the house. The forest slopes down towards the lake – Bogensee – which is scattered with leaves. Beeches, oaks and strips of damp, fern-covered marsh surround the small lake.

Autumn has fully turned and the lake glows with the colour of it. The water itself is brown, toffee-like and thick, and the air is thick too. Cold and damp, hanging heavily above the water. The creeping sadness of the house seems to have worked its way down here, as if the fear once manufactured in its rooms has penetrated the air of the place.

I step into the water and sink into the muck. The lake is full of eels, but I block out the thought of them and swim twenty feet out, to where I'm suspended in its opaque cold. Sam swims closer to shore, and then we both pick our way back to land and dry off. My fever has gone, but I don't quite feel well.

A few days later, fully recovered, I head out alone. I bike southwards, past Königs Wusterhausen, towards Großer Tonteich. It's a clear patch of water at the end of a gravel road near some allotments. Birch trees line its north shore and a campsite sits on the south. It's a thimble of a lake; *Teich* means pond. It feels safe, luminous, quiet.

The feeling of desolation from Bogensee has lifted. It's too easy to be sucked under by sadness in the autumn. The weather has been curling in towards winter, at one moment bright and at another grey and damp, but today is sunny. A single patch of thin cloud blows across the sky, and then the sky glows with the cold, white, late-October light. I swim out into it. The water temperature is exactly right for the air, bracing but not cold. The lake is clear and peaceful, so I linger a while, rolling on to my back, watching the leaves fall from the trees. I savour the lightness of it all, the watery feeling of suspension and the crisp glow of the sun.

schatz

A week into November, the pleasant weather has held over. These glimpses appear in autumn, bright patches of warmth spreading into the winter, a slight glow that convinces me it might never get cold. The darkness will come, though, and in a few months I won't quite be able to remember how bright these days have been. There's a rhythm to the light, and my moods move with it, a buoy on a rolling sea.

Last week at Großer Tonteich felt like an affirmation, a silent confirmation that the strength I had been building in September hadn't slipped away. I was beginning to find comfort not just in swimming alone, but in sharing it with others, and was learning how to switch between the two. I didn't know such a thing was possible. Most of my life, when I was with other people, I could only ever imagine continuing to be with them. I felt a desperate longing to melt myself down into them, and when they would leave the shock of reconstituting myself as a whole individual seemed a terrifying task. But in the end it was never as bad as I imagined it would be.

Walking helps. On my bicycle, I lose myself in speed, in the slick glide of the tyres on the road. My legs and the pedals become a single moving thing, spinning in time. Being back on my feet is different. At a walker's pace, everything changes: expanding and contracting. Distance stretches. The minutiae of the trail present themselves.

Swan's-neck thyme-moss – *Mnium hornum*, one of the most common mosses – appears. Its sporophytes reach into the minuscule, unseen upper atmosphere of the ground. The geology of the landscape underfoot vibrates into my feet.

It's at this pace that my mind quiets, and with the swing of my gait that I do most of my best thinking and writing. It's easy to retreat into my head on these walks. But I focus my attention: there's much to see. Mostly, I look for mosses.

I've become obsessed with mosses. The forests and the damp ground here are covered in them, thick blankets of green in every shade. Mosses are a steadying force: patient, sturdy, but soft. Mosses are masters of their tiny worlds, experts at making life in the boundary layer of their small environments. Without water, mosses simply curl into themselves, waiting. They can lose ninety-eight per cent of their moisture and still survive. This is why, if you've ever taken a cluster of moss home from a country walk, you can revive it months later. When water does come, the moss can make the best use of it. Being only one cell thick, every part of the moss is intimate with water.

But still, they are neglected. Bryology, the branch of study devoted to bryophytes – mosses, lichens and liverworts – is a rare specialism. Botanists prefer angiosperms, the flowering, seed-bearing array of plants that includes trees and herbaceous flowers. Most plants you know are probably angiosperms. Roses. Tomatoes. Daisies. Most of what we eat comes from angiosperms. They make up most of the plants I learned in my studies. Like many things, because they're the thing we know the most about, they're the thing people take the most interest in.

Bryophytes, on the other hand, ask me to slow down. I crouch down low to the ground. I meet them at eye level, at the level of their micro-environment. Larger mosses grow underwater. Some species of *Mnium*, related to the swan's-neck thyme-moss, grow in lakes. Evolutionarily somewhere between algae and land plants, mosses are the link between the water and the landscape.

When moss appears in a landscape, it is one of the first stages on the way to woodland. They are among the first things to arrive on bare ground, along with grasses and wildflowers. These eventually give way to scrub, shrubby plants that darken the surface of the ground. When young and fast-growing trees like birch arrive, strong woodland is not far behind. All of this can take over a century. In Brandenburg, the names of forests give a hint to the story of succession. Here, *Heide*, which normally means 'heath', usually refers to forest: pine forest grown over the spare, sandy heathland of the region. Moss is at the centre of such stories.

I've been writing about forest succession in my research, tracing the transformation of scrubby fields and hedgerows into full-blown woodland on Hampstead Heath. It's all I can think about. Looking at the margin of this German path now is like seeing a fragment of the wider timescale of ecological change.

Swan's-neck thyme-moss carpets the edge of the path I'm walking. I'm looking for water, north of the city again, finding a trail that runs through Birkenwerder, a small town with a quaint, red-tile-roofed town centre. The trail appears at the end of a residential street and is part of the 66-Seen-Wanderung, the 66-Lakes Trail, a four-hundred-kilometre-long hiking route that forms a ring around the city. Its name belies fact: the trail passes more than seventy lakes, but sixty-six was thought to be a nicer sounding number.

I've picked up sections of this trail throughout my swims: many of the lakes circling the city fall along its route. The trail markers – a blue circle in a white square – appear faded, painted on to trees in most of the forests around the city. Despite their haggard appearance, the trail isn't old.

Manfred Reschke, the author of my trail guide, now in his seventies, marked the trail some years after reunification. Reschke grew up in West Berlin. The world of water in Brandenburg was beyond the Wall, but West Berliners, unlike their Eastern neighbours, could cross the border by train, car or foot. Reschke, I learned, took to walking across and taking hiking trips throughout the Brandenburg countryside. The landscape that so many sought to leave was the very place he was headed. The 66-Seen-Wanderung is just one of the trails marked by him.

Today I plan to walk a ten-kilometre section of it,

repeating a walk I've done before that should, if all goes well, lead me to one of the best lakes I've known. The lake isn't on the trail, but hidden nearby, a treasure off the map. It's hard to find.

It starts with a marsh. Birch wood gives way to straight, skinny alder, sunken deep in the marsh along the River Briese, which cuts north of the city. A successional stage between swamp and forest, this *Erlenbruchwald* is known in English as a 'carr'. Like 'Berlin', 'carr' basically means 'swamp'.

The trail follows the river, winding its way sidelong across Brandenburg. It's a strip of dry ground amidst water: the carr is high in winter, with opaque, still water rising to the trunks of the alders. I imagine the sensation of water rising high around the trees, and it feels like hands wrapped around my waist, too intimate, too close. The carr is all sensation, swans moving silently between the trees, water glistening with an oily slickness. It's beautiful and repulsive at once.

I follow the trail eastwards to the end of the carr, where the trees begin to thin. Upriver from Birkenwerder is a series of grassy fields, desiccated swathes of gold amidst the marsh and plantation pines. It's unseasonably warm, and by the time the dirt trail opens on to a sunny sand track, it's noon. There's a white hot sun and no cloud. There is no one to be seen.

I follow the track – the brightness of the daylight reflected off the white sand – past a farmhouse from which I hear only roosters calling, the occasional cry in what feels like summer air. An electrical line running alongside me is buzzing where it meets the pylon. I find a rhythm in the sound, as I've found my rhythm in walking, and in the buzzing haze of the clearing I begin to sing to myself.

I was here a little over a year ago with Jacob. We'd walked for hours, searching for Lubowsee. He'd led us into a field lined with signs warning about wild boar, convinced the lake was at its other end. It was, but the Briese, which runs through the field, had turned the ground to marsh. We sank in up to our ankles. That was an unseasonably warm day too.

The German word for treasure is *Schatz*. I think of it as I'm walking, remembering that first visit to Lubowsee. It had been hot, and we were lost. The lake had receded from us in the heat, and appeared through the trees only once we'd given up. A single dock appeared out of nowhere, as if by magic, stretching out from the trees and over the lake. Seeing it, we ran towards it, throwing off our clothes, diving in. The water was bright and warm, as though its surface were stitched with gold leaf.

I'm looking for the dock again today, straining to remember the point in the pines where the trail branched off. I see the signs for the 66-Seen-Wanderung turning north, and I know this is where I leave the trail. Instead, I walk east, through a cathedral of pine. The trees form long corridors through the wood, and I follow one in what I remember is the direction of the lake. The trees become more errant here and begin to sway and creak above me. Despite the warmth, the sun sits too low in the sky to reach the ground, and I have the sensation of clawing my way through a dark wood in search of light. The earth is grown over with moss, and tiny skeletons of bilberry brush at my ankles. I begin to wonder if the lake was never really here, an optical illusion, a trick of my memory. Memory has begun to feel like a filter, a haze obscuring sight. But I know it's a lake that hides.

Without warning, the glint of golden light appears through the trees: the lake, and a few yards along, the dock. I walk out on to it and find it much the same as I'd left it last autumn, a single spider web stretched between the bars of the rusted ladder, vibrating in the air. I touch it with my fingertips and move it aside, peering over the edge into the water. The ladder's pattern of rust red and peeling white paint is exactly as I remember it.

I slip out of my clothes and climb down, lowering myself into the water, and swimming out backwards. It is a temperature between cold and cool, light on the skin. The water smells of grass and is the colour of butterscotch. Swimming here there's only the sound of my toes kicking at the surface, as if the lake is sheltered from the surrounding forest by the same magic that kept it hidden from view. I swim until my legs grow tired, then clamber back on to the dock, cold and exhausted. It feels as good today as it did a year ago. I breathe the sun in great gulps, then lie stretched on my back, grateful to be here alone.

Once I'd grown comfortable in Chocolate Lake, I'd begun exploring. The rocky landscapes inland from Halifax harbour were spotted with lakes, marine-blue patches of water edged with wild blueberry bushes. It wasn't a perfect solution. I would bike to William's Lake, half an hour outside of town, and find myself too terrified to get in. I'd sit on the rocks by the shore, dipping my feet in the cold.

The lake there was immediately deep, slipping directly off the edges of the rock and into the bottomless blue that had scared me as a child.

Once in a while, feeling brave, I would slide in and paddle near the rocks, staying in for no more than a minute. When I swam like that, I would stop breathing, as if it might hold the terror at a distance long enough for me to clamber back on to the rocks and back to safety. I did it again and again, unwinding the knots of terror.

I kept swimming in Chocolate Lake at night, leaving my clothes piled on the empty lifeguard station and swimming out into the black. On clear nights, the sky would be doubled around me, and the feeling of depth would turn into weightlessness, like I was floating in space. In the darkness, the border between water and air seemed to disappear, the sensation of the lake on my skin fleeing along with sight. The lake at night was like a vacuum, vacated of fear.

Night swimming became a small gift, a treasure I learned to reserve for the best days. They're rare. The summer before I first moved to Berlin, when I'd gone back to Halifax for my divorce, my friends and I walked for an hour to go night swimming in Chocolate Lake. I hadn't swum there in seven years, and I'd underestimated the length of the walk. We arrived exhausted, feet sore, in the middle of the night. It was freezing cold for August, but as we sat cross-legged and shivering, drying off by the lake, we all agreed it had been worth it.

Between Berlin lakes this August, I flew home to Canada to spend a week at the cottage with family. At night, the sky there is as black and clear as the lake. I spent the nights there swimming naked, floating on my back, watching the darkness. From the water's surface, the full curve of the Earth appeared, a stretching, star-streaked dome spinning overhead. It reminded me of those early days in Krumme Lanke, when I first arrived in Berlin. I lay still, searching for meteors.

The Perseids appear every August, flashing brightly across the sky as they burn up in our atmosphere. I've looked for them each summer since I was a teenager and suspect I always will. What we see isn't the meteoroid, but its burn: dust and ice singeing in the air, streaking brightly across the sky. I sometimes think their serendipitous flashes mark a stitch between our first record of them, two thousand years ago, and me. Ancient Chinese astronomers saw over a hundred of them, and their annual reappearance links us: them, in my maternal grandparents' lost homeland, and me, floating in the water. They link me to every summer that has passed.

As I lingered at the lake's surface, my black hair drifted into a fluid crown. The Milky Way stretched an icy glow across the night and the black of the lake swallowed me. Swaddled in darkness, there was only the sound of the water on my ears, and in the stillness I waited for shooting stars to light the seam between lake and sky.

grey

I wake up grey and weighty. I'd been up late the night before, watching the news of an attack unfold in Paris. The newscasters had talked over the gunfire footage, then panned to a shot of a single running shoe left on the pavement. Friends had checked in on Facebook, letting the digital world know they were safe. The real world seems small these days.

I roll over and see a message from my dad. He wants me to stay safe, it says, and to stay away from public places. He's thousands of miles away, watching the news, transmitting his worry across the ocean by fibre-optic cables sunken deep underwater. His worry reaches me in a bubble of grey on my phone, like a diver surfacing from the depths.

I don't want to stay home. I want to shake off this feeling of discomfort, so I pack my lunch and set out towards Alexanderplatz. It's empty for a Saturday morning, a few tourists strewn about snapping pictures of the Fernsehturm. I drift past them and into the station.

The train drops me in Rangsdorf, thirty kilometres south of the city. A busy road cuts the town in half: on one side sit rows of East German apartment blocks, and on the other side the sprawl of suburban houses and pine trees. It reminds me of the neighbourhood I grew up in, big houses with empty yards, pine trees marking the property lines. The air smells sweet, of smoke and pine resin.

I make my way down towards the lake and find it windswept and grey. November is nearing its end, winter rolling in. On the beach, a dozen or so men are standing in wetsuits, watching windsurfers and kitesurfers skid across the shallows. I wander over and ask in German if it would be okay to swim here.

'Yes, but it's cold, you know,' replies one of the men in perfect English, his hair still wet. He has peeled his wetsuit from his torso, and it hangs limply around his waist.

'I know,' I explain, annoyed at the change in language. I should work on my accent. 'I swim all winter.' He shrugs in reply, so I wander to the very edge of the beach, away from the surfers and up against a patch of reeds.

I strip off and step out into the water. The wind is working the lake into small, forceful waves, but I plough through them, walking towards its centre. Fifty yards out, the depth rises only to my knees, so I relent and lie down flat in the shallows. It's a lake so shallow that it risks deoxidising each summer; the kind of lake scientists call hypertrophic. Too many nutrients in too shallow a space. The fish here risk dying. When winter sets in, it will be a world of near solid ice.

I try to swim, but the rough wind sends cold water rushing into my mouth. I paddle awkwardly against the waves, but the shallowness of the water makes it difficult to float. It's too choppy, and the surfers are sliding ever closer, so I stand up again, frustrated, and make my way back to shore. The sensation of cold slips off my skin as I dry in the wind, and as I slip back into my clothes, I see the men across the beach shaking their heads, bemused.

The summer before my final year at university, I took to swimming in the sea. My rages softened and dissipated. The coast of Nova Scotia dipped southwards, curving in small grey crescents along the salty cold of the North Atlantic. Granite, slate and sandstone crackle across the landscape, making the ground rugged, sharp-edged like the air. It was always a bit cold, even in summer. The ocean would sting my legs as I swam, but I would wade out and stay afloat until my fingers were numb. The water calmed me. On the beach, I would dry in the wind and the sun, letting the salt form crystals in my hair.

One of those days, I went to the beach with the man who I would marry. He was eight years older than me, dark and moody and alluring, and I, at twenty, fell immediately in love. I hadn't felt anything like it before. I was shy and nervous around him. When he came to the coffee shop I worked at, I would hide behind the concrete wall and ask my colleagues to serve him. He told me later that he loved the way I became awkward and sweet with him, like he had softened my difficult edges into fluid curves. We were two unstable forces drawn together, but with him, I learned to become the steady one, the person who held things in place. He was the anchor I'd longed for.

We spent that summer making love, and then sitting

on the floor of his empty, unfurnished apartment, eating unsweetened cereal covered with maple syrup. We laughed and laughed, and then tried to sleep but had sex instead. I learned that he smelled of lavender, dry cotton and the sea. On long drives at night, listening to The Magnetic Fields, he held my hand when 'The Book Of Love' came on and would sing along in a comedic, low voice. We walked along the foggy arm of ocean that stretched around the city, listening to the floating buoy bells at night. The beginnings of our relationship were swaddled in that harbour fog, a moment of stillness before everything changed.

We're taking the S-Bahn north, up along the Havel towards Schulzendorf. Anne is with me; after our swim in the summer, she's offered to join me again. She wants to swim through winter, but has never made it past November. I've promised her that it'll be easy, so long as she keeps swimming regularly. In any case, I'm glad for the company.

The winter is settling over Berlin. The blustery weather from the other week has held over, and today the sky hangs low and spits fat, cold raindrops. Everything is grey.

The road from the S-Bahn station takes us westward, under a railway bridge and past a rusting condom machine, which Anne laughs at.

'It's so Brandenburg,' she says simply.

We follow the road through the suburbs, past houses still sleeping through Sunday morning. A kilometre along, we come to an enormous allotment, one of Berlin's many *Kleingärten* designed to provide city dwellers with access to outdoor space. Next door is an FKK sports club, outside of which a flag waves, painted with a golden figure leaping over a globe. A naturist sauna and sports club, it's one of the many cultural relics of the East, sitting quietly next to the allotment. Anne tells me about her childhood in the West, about holidays in France where she swam naked in the sea. West Germans are known for the same prudishness as the English and Americans, but she didn't grow up that way, she says. I peer through the fence of the sport club. It's empty.

We follow the lane through the allotments. They're the most perfectly formed gardens I've seen: tiny, tile-roofed houses set into small lawns, paved roads lined with iron street lamps. Everything is near miniature, almost life-sized but not big enough for every day. Their low gates are mostly locked.

The fences of the gardens back on to the lake, and we're looking for a way in. Around the eastern side, there's a small beach, but it's padlocked and lined with barbed wire. Heiligensee is a private lake, with access restricted to those who own lake-shore property. I ask Anne if she's okay with trespassing, and she laughs.

'Of course, that's why I'm here!' she says brightly.

We wind our way back to the gardens and hoist ourselves up over the steely grey fence. Its slats are narrow, so Anne takes off her shoes and passes her bag overtop. On the other side, it's another world: wind-blown water and a quiet dock. Shiny steel ladders dip down into the grey.

We pile our clothes in the order we'll put them on in. When your hands are stiff with cold, preparation means everything. Stripped down to my swimsuit, I climb down off the dock and into the water. As I swim out, the grey of the lake appears black, clear and clean but immeasurably deep, overwhelmingly cold. I can't stay in long; the winter has arrived, and I swear into the wind. The pain slides down my ankles and into my feet. My fingertips grow thick and clumsy with numbness. Thin, spitting rain blows across the lake's surface.

I clamber back out into the wind and dry off, cold pleasure spreading across my back, watching Anne swim. She swims out a way, with none of the profanities and complaints that accompanied my swim. She's tougher than me, I think; she handles the cold a little better. A good friend to have around as winter widens ahead of me.

Part way through that last year at university in Nova Scotia, I was accepted on to a post-graduate course in London and began making plans to leave Canada. I was going to a land I chose for myself: small, rolling, and eternally green. My parents worried. It was a place I was never meant to go back to, as if back-tracking in our family history was the ultimate transgression. At the time, none of that crossed my mind; I worried about my relationship, about him.

I threw myself into work again, and as my plans began to materialise, my boyfriend decided to come with me. I would study and find some part-time work, and he would begin his career. Relieved, I packed my things and moved to London. He followed a few weeks later.

On that small island, the winter barely spread its breath across the south. When the crocuses peeked through in February, it was still glowing green. There was dampness there, but it afforded a kind of beauty, a cloak of mossy green across the crumbling brick terraces. We moved from a tiny rented flat in Kentish Town to a larger flat in Dartmouth Park, near Hampstead Heath. It had a broken window, but it also had crown mouldings and a shining marble fireplace, so we loved it. It had a view over the garden, our small patch of green in the grey city. We walked across the Heath every night after dinner, every night passing the same old man with a pug which clutched in its mouth an enormous ball. The man sat on the bench waiting for his dog to catch up to him; we laughed about it every night, eating ice cream, holding hands. It was good for a while.

We got married – a paper act – when I was twenty-three, and from then on I tethered myself to the ship's mast of our relationship, like Ulysses, like Turner. I watched our relationship unfold itself, unable to do anything about it. He retreated into a place inside himself, neither softness nor hard work could fix it. He drank, and he disappeared. I began to wonder if this was the same person I'd loved back in Nova Scotia, the man who had smelled of lavender and the sea.

I learned that I couldn't fix someone else. I just had to decide how long I was willing to wait. That little flat near the Heath housed both our marriage and the small piece of adulthood that I plastered over the years we spent together, falling apart.

I'd attempted to make a new life. I'd moved far from family, and bound myself to my decision as if it couldn't be undone. I felt too ashamed to undo it.

My father visited and laughed scornfully at the terraced houses – dark down the middle with only windows on the ends, he said – and I knew it was because he'd grown up in one, across the borderland, land of my father. The tidal inflow of the Severn had kept him from England. When the new bridge from Wales was finally finished in 1966, he'd cycled its length the morning before the opening ceremony, staking claim, marking territory before the cars would rush over it, fuller than the tide. It was a tiny betrayal, my boarding a plane and ending up in England, unceremoniously. I didn't take it seriously at the time.

waiting

I'm biking east from Königs Wusterhausen when I hit the sand track. It runs into the forest as far as I can see, forming a thin, white margin between a scattering of pine stands and farm fields. I look at my map, frustrated, but it's the best way through. I apologise to my bicycle and push on.

The track runs for seven kilometres from the small village of Senzig down towards Frauensee – 'Women's Lake' – where I want to swim. It takes forever, and at every mound of thick sand I hop off my bike and walk for a bit, gazing up at the sky's patch of sun and cloud. I set out late today and hope the daylight lasts long enough for a swim.

It's December. Winter is arriving in patches: cold winds and grey skies, dark evenings swaddling the city streets. The brightness of this weekend is an anomaly, and I want to take it in, to take the light and the air into my lungs and hold them there until spring. Winter will bring its own pleasures – the ice especially – but sunshine is rarely one of them.

When I reach the lake, I follow a footpath eastwards, searching for the best spot to swim. It's lined with reeds, and the far end of the lake peters out into sloping, scrubby banks and then rows of pine. On this side of the water, however, it's sparse. Light reaches the ground in pale shafts through the gaps in the trees, mostly oaks. Sound carries over the lake too, voices chattering away. Ahead of me, there's a group of elderly walkers clad in puffy winter jackets. One of them wears a Santa hat. They're all carrying mistletoe out of the woods, approaching the campsite and youth centre nearby. A holiday fair is in full force, and the sounds of music are echoing through the trees. Christmas is coming soon.

I duck off the path behind them, watching them disappear towards the campsite, and carry on looking for a place to swim. Ahead of me I see a beach, so I rest my bicycle on its side and approach the water's edge. It's clear and sandy, and an unused dock stretches out along the edge of the reeds. Stripping down and stepping in, I find the water brisk but not too cold; some lakes seem to hold the heat better than others. Frauensee feels exactly right. I swim out on my back, but the sun is beginning to sink below the tree-line and shadow creeps over the beach. The scent of wood smoke carries across the air, out on to the water, curling in towards evening. Dry warmth calling me back to shore.

The years I spent married had the opposite of their intended effect: a relationship designed to bring two people together instead taught me to be on my own, incrementally. I felt as though I'd spent those years holding my breath, swept under by some current that would grab hold again whenever I neared the surface. Intimacy had disappeared, touch and affection dissolved, and with them any willingness to try.

I carried on as if we'd been married much longer than we had: I worked and shopped and cooked in routine. We went to a hole-in-the-wall Thai restaurant in Tufnell Park every Thursday night, when we were both home early from work, and the woman in the restaurant came to know us by the enormous bottle of water we ordered. We chatted to her, and she watched us quietly eating in the empty restaurant. I sometimes think she was one of the only witnesses to our marriage. When it ended, many of my friends said they were never convinced he'd existed. We'd spent those years as if in hiding.

I spent my time approximating some half-formed idea of daily life. While he worked gruelling contracts in social care, falling apart within himself and disappearing into drink, I worked most days at my job for an educational charity and three evenings a week pulling pints for bankers in a city pub. The recession had taken hold, so there were a lot of pints to pour.

On Friday afternoons I did the shopping. On Saturdays I went to the farmers' market, and on Sundays I cooked a proper dinner. When he stopped eating what I'd cooked, I continued anyway, as if I thought that my own steadiness, my own stillness might catalyse a change. Or at least, it wouldn't get worse. My denial was as complete as his retreat from me. The uneaten meals stacked up next to the kitchen sink.

After two years I'd grown tired, and having spent

most of that time living with a shadow of a relationship, a shadow of a partner, I no longer feared being alone. I realised that I'd been doing it all along.

I took to running. The summer our marriage ended I ran hard and fast across Hampstead Heath, damp clay soaking my ankles. I ran up Swain's Lane past Highgate Cemetery, up the brick-lined hill and back down again. I ran to the Ladies' Pond on the Heath. I hadn't been swimming much in those years.

That pond ought to have scared me; it would have, some years earlier. With a concrete dock and two ladders dipping straight down into the deep, there was no halfway point. No beach, no shallows. Just depth.

We had once taken a holiday in Santorini – when we still believed things were fixable – and had swum off the back of a boat in the middle of the Caldera. I'd hung off the edge of the ladder, hesitating, terrified, but he had treaded water next to me. He stayed with me, watching as I dipped down slowly into the clear sea, panicking as I swam. He never left my side that day.

The Ladies' Pond wasn't like that. I began to swim there alone, surrounded by women who seemed stronger than me. I wanted to be like them: sturdy, no-nonsense, unsentimental. The pond was opaque and slipped around my body thickly, the water a felted brown. It was cold and open: a bright circle of relief in the middle of the trees. I swam out into its centre again and again, out towards the willow and then back towards the dock. I swam to the lane rope at its farthest edge, watching the cormorants glide through the deep. The movement was an anaesthetic.

Leaving my marriage meant leaving my home: the flat near the Heath, the routine, the city. I'd been offered a scholarship to do a doctorate in Toronto. A way out, a plan. It came at exactly the right time, and though I didn't want to leave, and didn't want to return to Canada, I knew I had to take it. I was only twenty-four, and it was an opportunity to repair my life, to learn to stand steadily and alone.

I remember the taxi ride to the airport on the day I left. I remember looking around our empty rooms, the marble fireplace bare, my suitcases at the door. I remember locking my keys inside the flat, and then watching the terraced houses slip away as the taxi drove. We never drove past the Heath, so I didn't get to watch it slip away.

The day after Frauensee is even brighter, so I decide to take another swim – this time in Butzersee. I'm out on my bike early, before the park fills with families taking in the December sun. I'd woken up from a fitful sleep, a handful of hours scrabbled together late in the night. Another dissertation deadline is approaching, and for the most part, sleep has been eluding me for weeks. Instead, I've taken to walking in one of Berlin's nineteenth-century municipal parks, Volkspark Friedrichshain, at night. Most nights, there's clear darkness but occasionally a fine mist gathers around the tree trunks, tiny droplets of water suspended in the air. The border between dry land and the world of water is a porous one. Each night I trace the same route through the park, chain-smoking cigarettes, and then go home and sit on my bedroom floor working, like I did when I was at university. I worry I'm slipping back into old habits. When I'm not biking or swimming, only walking and work keep my nervous energy at bay.

I feel awake in the bright sunlight, though, and as I draw my bike down Karl Marx Allee I'm smiling. I have the road to myself; Berlin is quietest on Sundays. Stores stay shut. There isn't much to do. This early, I can slip out of the city unnoticed, swim, and be back before breakfast.

I cycle on towards the lake, one of the three lakes out near Kaulsdorf, where I swam in the summer. I've been longing for this lake, waiting for exactly the right day. It's incredibly clear and open, laid across a field south-east of the city, dug from a former quarry. When I arrive, the flat emptiness of the lake is a mirror, the sun doubled in the sky and water, too bright to look at. I pull my hat down over my ears – despite the sun, it's still winter – and put on my sunglasses.

My ankles sense the cold first, the kind of clear pain that hits your bones but not your skin. Within seconds, though, the feeling abates and I can walk out into the lake, plunging to my neck. I swim out towards the sun, squinting behind my sunglasses, and tread water in the middle of the lake. The water in winter is stratified, clear as in the early summer, and as I circle my legs in the cold I can see my toes and the receding depth beneath them. It's still December, though, so I can't stay in too long. I pull myself back to the shore, long strokes in the sun, and scrabble back on to the sand.

By the time I'm dressed, the cold of the swim has gone. I sit in the sun eating my breakfast as dog walkers appear on the path. One woman stops, looks at me.

'*Waren Sie baden?*' she asks. Were you swimming? She sounds incredulous. It's a question I'll hear again and again, every time I meet a passerby during the winter. I tell her yes, and she looks horrified, then walks on, shaking her head.

'Freedom is the negotiation of ghosts on a haunted landscape; it does not exorcise the haunting but works to survive and negotiate it with flair.' I was sitting in the library, racing to the bottom of a stack of books, facing a deadline. But these words stopped me. I paused, traced my way back to the beginning of the sentence, and began again. 'Freedom is the negotiation of ghosts on a haunted landscape' – I mouthed the words, running my fingertip over the page. Maybe this was it. Each time I had moved somewhere new, to a new country or a new city, I soon found only the past in the present. There was a choice: keep moving or learn to live with ghosts. *Freedom*, it said. This seemed a promising thought.

The words appeared in the middle of a study on mushrooms by Anna Tsing, an anthropologist I've come to admire very much. That this academic study might provide the words my heart so needed seemed improbable, but they were there on the page, and then in my fingers as I diligently typed them up. I needed to take them with me.

After my marriage, I launched myself into work. I spent the next five years in archives and in the field, at work on my doctorate, as if returning to the scene might somehow repair it. As a historian, I spent those years chasing down ghosts in the landscape: those of my past and the pasts of others unknown to me, but everything I found seemed to recede just out of reach. I would find some fragment of the past, some story to tell, and it would somehow exceed itself. Words I wrote couldn't capture them; they evaporated like mist from the morning hillside, still there, but diffuse, in the air, no longer solid. Ghosts are like that: with you always, but not entirely yours and impossible to capture in your hands or in a story. I tried to get them into words anyway.

I hadn't wanted to leave the Heath, and my doctorate became a way of trying very hard to stay. The months I've spent finding my way across the flat plains of Brandenburg feels much the same. The unwinding of tension as I work my way from lake to lake. Getting to grips with ghosts.

The warmth is short-lived. The middle of December hangs damply in the weeks before Christmas. It's the worst kind of cold – almost English cold, wet and pervasive. I'd almost always prefer the snow.

I wake up angry. I've been working constantly, still not sleeping, and bristle at every comment from friends about my habits, about my moods. I worry that I'm growing isolated, difficult to be around. With work pressure closing in, I've grown uneasy, unkind. When I'm not writing or swimming, I lie swaddled in my duvet, watching Netflix, eating takeaway Thai food. I'm hoping it will pass, that it's just winter settling on me.

My choice of lake doesn't help. I hate Plötzensee. Many Berliners love it. In summer the beach here is packed, riotous on a weekend. But all I see is the stretch of industrial waste on the way to the lake. I feel only the furious wind as I push my bike along the canal. Then the lake appears and I remember that it's fenced off on this side, that I need to slip under the chain-link and scrabble down to its frowning shore.

I can't quite place what I find so grim about Plötzensee. Anne suggests that it might be the history: the Plötzensee prison is nearby, where political prisoners were held, sentenced to hard labour and executed under the Nazi regime. North of the lake is a cemetery. This corner of the city feels crowded despite its starkness. There is a kind of sunken quality to the place – indeed, local legend says that a village here was once swallowed by the rising lake of Plötzensee. But it may also just be my mood, the darkening grey of the winter.

I lock my bike to the fence and slide under, my backpack snagging on the fence's coiled edges. The shore-line is ragged, litter working its way into the ground, and the water moves in slate grey waves. Thin rain begins to fall.

I'm going to make this quick – in and out, a final swim before I slip off to see family in Canada for the holidays. The promise of a break from work is the one steady thing on my horizon. My best friend Rachel is turning thirty and we've planned a weekend away with friends before we all shuttle off for family Christmases. The past weeks in Berlin have felt leaden as I've waited to go back. I've missed my close friends more than ever these past months.

I slip into the water and it's exactly as I expect: bracing cold, the metallic feeling of its grey sliding over me. I swim out into the centre, counting my strokes, longing to be out and dry again. I count to sixty and then turn back. Better things await me in the days ahead: warmth, light and respite from the grey of the city. When I come back, I hope it will have turned to white.

winter

Stratification: As the water cools below four degrees, the coldest layer floats to the top, eventually forming ice. The water directly beneath the ice remains at four degrees. The ice shields the lake from wind, so the layers remain stratified.

under ice

The air is algid. January brought full winter with it: the snow and then the ice. Anne and I tread carefully as we descend the frozen stairwell between the S-Bahn station and Schlachtensee. A sticky white snow coats the ground. The lake ahead is glassy and white.

I've packed a hammer, and as I walk it clinks against the side of my thermos, a promise of warmth. Anne tells me about her Christmas holidays as we walk, our words forming thin clouds of water vapour in the air ahead of us. She had been swimming back home on the western edge of Germany, before the ice arrived. I'd been in the Great Lakes. My sister had swum with me in Lake Erie. My father had driven me to Lake Huron and watched from the shore, calling me crazy, a trace of admiration in his voice. It had been nice to be back home, but I longed also for Berlin. I've become divided, stretched across places.

Now, back in Berlin, we tuck ourselves into a small clearing on the lake's southern edge. There's a patch of liquid water twenty feet out, and I think the ice here is thin enough to carve through. Anne looks sceptical – it's her first winter – but I'm determined. I strip off my clothes and step towards the ice, wielding my small household hammer.

There's a sound made by ice when you hammer into it. First, a chipping, as you hit the hard surface and it breaks away like glass. Then the dry, bristling sound of the surface nearby crackling as the force of the hammer ripples through it. The ice sheet begins to move and break up. The twinkling sound of the lake emerging from its icy cap is like a far-off rustling, someone standing at a distance crumpling a piece of cellophane.

I chip a hole large enough to stand in, and from there I step barefooted into the cold – the water at one degree Celsius – and begin to hammer my way out towards the lake's centre. It's a numbing cold, pain gleaming into my bones and then retreating, and within a few seconds I'm comfortable, able to stand for the few minutes it takes me to unpick a seam in the ice sheet. Tiny fragments of ice gather around my legs, thin as flakes of glass, and I push them aside, under the water, under the frozen cap of the lake. I know that later, when I dry off, these thin flakes will have left tiny cuts all over me, as deft as paper, minuscule slices in my skin. It's a small price.

I'm waist-deep, and the ice is growing thinner as the lake deepens. Fifteen feet out, the sheet ahead of me relents and breaks apart, and a clear path opens between the shore and the open water. I turn and call for Anne to swim out.

She hasn't swum with ice before, and when she steps in a deep exhalation of voice and breath leaves her. It's painful the first time, but I'm out in the deep now, enveloped in the black cold of the lake. The sharp paroxysms of pain have ceased in me, but I watch them work their way over Anne as she swims out. Between pain and numbness there's a brightness, a crisp, heightened sensation in the cold: that's the place to swim through. When it ends, when numbness arrives, it's time to get out.

I wade back to shore and slide up the snowy ridge, on to a towel that stiffens with slick ice as I step dripping on to it. The water beads on my skin and disappears in the dry air. As I dress, bright whispers of sensation slip across my back and arms, like a thousand hands touching the surface of my body. This sensation is the reason why I hammered out into the lake. This brief but intense moment of physical pain, then pleasure, followed by total elation: the cold catalyses an endorphin rush.

Schlachtensee, Anne reminded me earlier, means 'Battle Lake'. My German isn't good enough to catch every nuance, and I'd missed that one. But back on the shore, dry and still shaking with cold, I think about my hammer, about the ice, and about the brief but uncontainable torment I'd sought in the water.

When I started winter swimming I became obsessed with the ice. With the colour of it – that clear white-blue – and the sensation of it as I ran my fingers across its surface, slick and numbing. For some time, ice had been on the minds of people around me: scholars in environmental research, scientists grappling with melting glaciers and rising sea levels. I'd grown up with it – the persistent freeze of Canadian winter – but the very materiality of ice had seemed far-off, an alien thing belonging to the North or to the Antarctic, not yet to me. I went to conferences on landscape and all anyone could talk about was ice. Scientists from the British Antarctic Survey showed their maps, artists played video loops of melting ice. The cold was everywhere in our warming world.

Ice holds stories. To the German Romantics, *Eisblumen* – the patterns of frost that scale windowpanes on cold days – spoke to matters of both life and death. Likened to flowers by the German poet Karl Ludwig von Knebel, the ephemeral frost patterns were the subject of intense debate in aesthetic and scientific exchanges between Knebel and the poet Goethe. Did the *Eisblumen*'s intricate patterning derive from a relationship with organic life? The ice flowers – like stones and crystals bearing the orderly patterns found in nature – could be said to hold stories about the world, about life. But as is the case with ice, *Eisblumen* are temporary. As solid as we think ice to be, it disappears: phenomena like ice flowers are reminders of this.

The long distant past is brought into the present through melting ice. In the nineties, receding glaciers in the ice fields at the Alaskan–Canadian border revealed bear hides, hunting tools, relics of life from eight thousand years ago. Some years later, the frozen remains of a fifteenth-century hunter were uncovered in the territory of the Champagne-Aishihik First Nation. With him were found robes and tools scientists were keen to examine, more stories to be woven into the oral tradition of the local community. The glacier held all of this.

Entire worlds lie frozen beneath ice. In the past decade,

scientists have been digging into Antarctic glaciers to reach new lakes: dark, unseen, subglacial worlds. These aren't the glassy waters I find under January lake ice, but places of perpetual cold. They're time capsules containing fragments of a lost past, a past before we irreparably changed our world. When a team of researchers drilled eight hundred metres through a glacier to reach the shallow water of Lake Whillans – one of hundreds of subglacial lakes on the southern pole – they found life in the water, life in the mud. Single-celled organisms that survive in the darkness, feeding off of carbon dioxide. The Antarctic lakes are a world without phototrophic life, a world without sunshine, but life is there. The ice holds the world in wait.

When I'm not swimming, I read about these lakes endlessly. I watch videos about them online, longing for their white-blue ice, as if the cold on the screen might reach me. I watch sterile-suited scientists drill into the lake, past clear, pristine water. What the drill brings up is the mud, not what I imagine. A pristine muck, clots of the earth, like the knot in my chest I have been trying to unwind by swimming. It isn't untouched, but rather intimately touched – by time, by darkness, by the cold. It is intensely populated with life, held beneath the water and the ice sheet. The lakes around Berlin arrived here slowly, through glaciers, and it is as if the water's yearly retreat into solidity is a bridge between these cold places.

The winter is holding fast on to the city. In town, the Spree is solid, a clouded white block expanding between the embankments. The muddy tracks of toboggans line the hillsides. For a short burst, everyone is outside, and then just as quickly it is night and the city is too cold to bear.

A day as bright as summer arrives, a cold but glowing sun sitting high in the sky, and we set out. Coco and I take the S-Bahn east, past the city's edge and into Strausberg, thirty kilometres out, halfway to the Polish border. It's an old fortress town with a crumbling wall cutting through its centre. Straussee, where I swam in the summer, sits to its west.

We're not here for Straussee, but rather to walk the forest that stretches out beyond it, out towards Bötzsee. A thin layer of ice seals the path, so that I have to dig my heels into the ground with every step to avoid slipping. The sun leaves a thin layer of meltwater on the path. The snow clings to the ground stickily, noisily. Rounding Straussee, we come to the edge of the forest, white and green broken only by the burnt orange of the tree trunks. A single line of deer tracks extend into the woods; no other footsteps follow them, but we do.

In Fontane's *Rambles*, he wrote about summer in this forest and the one north of it, now merged as the Strausberger und Blumenthaler Wald. *Blumen* is the word for 'flower', for 'blossom', and Fontane thought the forest was so rich with blossom that it seemed to proclaim its own identity at every turn. 'I am the Blumenthal!' he wrote. Now, in winter, it remains alive in the absence of blossom: glowing green in the undisturbed snow, patches of moss brimming on the branches. The farther in we trek, the warmer it feels, as if something of summer was contained here between the trees and above the snow.

Coco and I are debating our superpowers – I can't decide whether I'd rather be able to withstand extreme cold or be good with a hatchet, as if they're mutually exclusive – when we arrive at Bötzsee. It's frozen solid, a blue-white seal of ice on the surface. It is thick, unmoving.

I'd been here last winter on my own, when the snow was just as sticky, and found the forest melting around me. The lake then had broken up into thick slabs of ice, like paving stones afloat in pools of shallow water. But today is entirely different: the cold hasn't abated and the lake, shallow as it is, has frozen fast to its edges, like the water has turned to stone. It doesn't move when I step out on to it, and as I test its thickness with the back of my hammer, I realise that swimming will be an impossibility. It's at least three inches thick.

I persist, anyway, working with my hammer over a piece of ice an arm's length away from me. It takes six blows with the back of the hammer to break a crack in the ice, an opening no wider than a coin. I keep going, creating a line of holes next to one another, until a small arc of open water appears. I'm perched on the edge of the frozen lake as I hammer, my heels resting on a tree root jutting out from shore, my toes on the ice. It isn't secure, and I should know better.

Coco watches from shore as the ice begins to break up. I heave great chunks of it aside as the hole widens, holding the fragments up to the light. It is heavy, but held against the light I think it is the clearest thing I've ever seen, incongruously light and fluid for its weight. Fresh water produces this kind of clarity; it's called 'sweet-water ice', from the German word *Süßwasser*, meaning fresh water. I throw the pieces aside and they clack and slide across the surface of the lake. Just as quickly, the ice beneath my feet gives way, and I fall sideways, clumsily, into the cold. My boots fill with water and slush, and I turn to see Coco laughing and then running towards me, her face torn between amusement and concern. I begin to laugh too.

She draws me out of the water, which is only waist-deep, and I lope sodden on to the shore. The hole in the ice is considerably larger now, I notice, before turning to my soaked clothes. I'll need to lay them out to dry before we take the long hike back through the snow. I strip off my leggings and lie them in the sun – I hadn't thought to bring a change of clothes and now realise my mistake – and tip my boots upside down to drain. I peel the socks off my feet and lay them side by side, curled and damp. I return to the ice with my hammer.

Stepping into the lake again, I plunge up to my waist. At the very least, a few more minutes with the hammer will give me enough space to move, though I'll never get a proper swim. Hammering away, my arms grow warm with the work of it as my legs grow cold in the water. Soon, the opening is five feet across and I'm able to stretch out into it, to luxuriate in the sensation of pain that washes over my limbs. The hammer rests on the ice as I sink down low into the lake, letting the cold work its way up my shoulders and around my neck.

Coco takes a photograph. When I look at it later, all I'll see is that damned hammer sitting next to me on the ice, a tiny crook of black steel atop the vastness of the frozen lake, this tiny thing I use to create a space for myself in the water. The lake around me is an unending white.

errare

Five months after first moving to Berlin, shortly after that trip to Rügen and the Baltic Sea with Jacob and Tom, I was scheduled to move back to London. Three years had passed since I'd left my husband and my life there. I'd spent most of that time in Toronto, at work on my doctorate. I'd grown stable, studious and stronger than I'd ever been. The flare-ups of my past had disappeared, and I no longer felt driven by fear. But I still longed for England.

The short time carrying out research in Berlin was always meant to be temporary, a grace period between the stages of the life I'd planned. I hadn't intended to love Berlin, and I hadn't intended to fall in love. I was a planner; the plan dictated what came next. My research position in Berlin had ended, and there was work to do on my doctorate. It was time to go back to England.

London was home: not simply because it had been home with my husband, but because it was something I chose and chose again. In all the years I'd been away, the magnetic grasp of the city hadn't disappeared. None of the other places felt like that: it felt as though the other places were things that just happened to me. I was born in Canada, I was sent to Berlin, all of that accidental. But I wanted to be back in London – amidst the greying streets and the frowning commuters – and I wanted to be near to the Heath again.

My friend Amy had a room for me in Shepherd's Bush, in the shadow of the Westfield Centre. It was on the top floor of a Victorian terrace with painted floorboards and a window overlooking the garden. It was quiet and mine. Arriving there, I felt relief, like I'd finished something I had set out to do. I'd found my way back to the city.

I climbed the stairs to my room and began to unpack. Unzipping my duffel, a card slipped out. It read: *1. Keep in touch. 2. Plan adventures with me. 3. Come back.* I realised then that Jacob had tucked it into my bag before I'd left, this small but captivating piece of him and our Berlin. I had left, tried wholeheartedly to put my feelings aside, but the card held a gravitational pull.

I'd been single-minded about returning to London for so long; the absence of the city had become a part of me, an invisible ache that had abated once I'd returned. Now in its place I felt some small fragment of something else: a longing for some other place, for this other person. But I resolved to be where I was, to make London home again, and to trust that in doing so, the feeling would dissipate.

There was work to do: I needed to finish my dissertation fieldwork, a long list of interviews I'd arranged as part of my research. I had a list of archives to visit. And I needed part-time work. My scholarship was paid in Canadian dollars and would barely cover the rent in London. The lightness of returning came with the shadow of financial pressure, of work, and of responsibilities I'd let slide back in Berlin. I had hoped it would be simple.

The day after returning, I stepped forward into a crossing on Oxford Street and was struck. I felt only the weight of the thing, heavy but hollow metal, and then nothing. There was a hard crack as I hit the road. There was a gap, a moment empty of all sensation, and then I was on my feet again, searching for the pavement. A crowd of strangers took my arms and sat me back down, slowly shuffling me on to the side of the road. Someone retrieved my glasses – somehow intact – from the middle of the intersection, and then I could see again. My vision was narrow, just a fragment of the night directly in front of me. I saw rain and traffic lights, the legs of the passersby not stopping. My ears rang with the electro-fuzz of fear, of adrenaline. To my left, a taxi driver had pulled over and was calling an ambulance. A sensation of heavy weight pressed on my right shoulder – the opposite of the lightness I felt in the water.

There was a familiar voice: Amy was with me, and her voice emerged from the din of rush-hour traffic. She was speaking to a man – a street cleaner – as he began to wrap me in a bin bag, as if it would keep me warm or dry. He slipped a bin bag under me and wrapped one around my shoulders, like I'd just run a marathon and needed to be wrapped in foil. I don't remember anyone's faces; I remember their legs and the cold feeling of the wet road. My first clear thought was of Jacob, about the words on the card.

When you swim in the cold, the pain triggers an endorphin rush that hits you moments after leaving the water. Initially, there's just shock. It can be incredibly dangerous – it can leave you gasping for breath. You risk swallowing water and drowning. But once the shock passes – and with it, the initial pain – there's space for something else. I feel it on my body when I step out of the cold and into the air: the sudden tightening of the skin as the water evaporates, the rush of sensation working its way across my body. There's the rush, the elation. It's an inexplicable lightness.

That same rush hit me after the accident. As I lay strapped to a spinal board in an ambulance, I told jokes to the paramedics. I laughed at my bad luck, returning to London and being immediately knocked down by a taxi. They asked if I had looked the wrong way, and then they put an oxygen tube to my mouth, and laughed along with me. They leaned in and told me not to be afraid, that they were wheeling me through the trauma unit. I smiled and told them I'd be fine. I was dazed, exaltation running through my limbs. Pain still throbbed, distantly now, in my shoulder. I looked over and saw Amy, anxiously clutching my bag in the corner of the ambulance.

The winter comes imperfectly. The elation of the ice isn't an unqualified pleasure: there are long days out, days when my phone grows so cold that it switches off and I find myself lost in the woods, still wondering why I haven't bought a paper map. Soon into January, a painful itching in my feet arrives – chilblains – and I spend nights awake sliding my toes against one another, trying to relieve the burning sensation. My big toes turn perpetually red, swollen, near blistered. I rub them with a mixture of black pepper and sesame oil – a home remedy that brings momentary relief but leaves me smelling like Chinese food. None of the pain seems enough to stop me swimming.

It's Friday. I'm wearing my parka, clumsily riding my bike with my woollen mittens on. It's minus ten degrees Celsius. I'm wearing sunglasses too, because the sky is so clear and so bright, with an enormous cold sun shining at its edge. The trees cast shadows in the snow that are pale blue, the same colour as the sky. It's promising.

Groß Glienicker See sits on the western edge of the city, nine kilometres from Spandau, at the very top of Sacrower See. They sit next to one another, one atop the other, like the dot and apostrophe that make up a semi-colon. I loved Sacrower See, so I have high hopes.

I cycle to the lake, slipping slowly along the peripheral residential lanes that are slick with ice. At the edge of the water, I stop. White snow dusts its surface. It's frozen entirely and so beautifully bright I don't want to touch it.

There's a small beach ahead, and two young men tracing broad curves on the ice. Hockey – though I've never played it, never watched it, and genuinely don't know the rules – makes me feel at ease. One of the small inheritances of being Canadian; it doesn't mean much to me personally, but it's a thing I'm meant to identify with, and at this point that's enough. Rachel once tried to teach me the rules, sitting in front of the television in our rented flat-share. She quizzed me on teams, on the meaning of 'power play'. Later, in England, I learned to call it 'ice hockey', but that has never felt right to me.

I stop with my bike and watch them skate, the alien,

elastic sound caused by their blades bouncing across the open lake. As the skaters move across it, it stretches and cracks. A frozen lake is always alive. The vibrating, tugging sound seems to affirm this. Skates slide across the ice, and everything moves just a little, like a loosely strung guitar strum, but more remote, more inexplicable. It's the sound of the ice cracking, but as sound travels it arrives in pieces from the nearest part of the ice first, and then the farthest, bouncing to the ear. In some places the sound is called 'ice yowling' or 'ice banshee', terms that capture its haunting, resonant twang. It haunts the lake in winter.

I walk out on to the ice and crouch down low, touching it with my bare fingertips. It's like rough glass, flecked with frost, and beneath it I can see the water, like seeing through the back of a mirror. Sweet water. Beneath my feet, a cluster of water starwort presses itself against the ice, green against glass, a winter bloomer. I watch its frozen, suspended stillness – alive in the cold – and watch for the lake's movement.

I can't swim here today. Not because of the ice's thickness – in some places it isn't so thick, and I have my hammer. I crave the cold, and having cycled all the way here am so keenly awaiting it. But I haven't made it here first. The hockey players are focused – they don't even look up when I walk out on to the lake. I don't think it is thick enough for skating, but I'm not going to make matters worse. Hammering into the ice, even at its edge, can compromise it much farther along the line. It splits and quakes itself in uncertain places, like cracks along a wall. And more than that, the silent sound of bright sun on snow, on the frozen lake, and that otherworldly sound of the skaters – I don't want to disturb them. The sound they make is already the sound of the ice breaking.

I take small, silent steps on the lake. Fifty feet out, there's an old couple. The man's breath clouds beneath a dark grey moustache, and the woman wears a woollen scarf one might more rightly call a blanket. They're huddled close to one another, walking. I've grown so accustomed to the cold. Stopping, they ask me how thick I think the ice is and, in my halting German, I surmise that it is probably ten centimetres thick. Not thick enough, I say, and they nod, glancing at the skaters. We all keep walking anyway.

I make my way back to shore and retrieve my bike, its bell frozen over with a thin frost. The entire road is frozen too, but I cycle back along it, minding the slickest patches, until I'm near the top of the lake. I step off to look at the lake here, and as I wheel my bike towards it I lose my footing and slide, bike and all, eight feet down a small hill. I land sideways atop my bicycle, hot breath knocked out of me, my knee hurting fiercely, momentarily. But I get up and continue, brushing the snow off me – it is cold, I can't feel much of anything anyway.

The sun is beginning to dip low in the sky, time to cycle back. Without the light, the temperature is dropping. In German, they say *arschkalt*. Arse cold. It sounds sharper, more cutting in German. I say it aloud and then repeat other swear words to cut the sting of the cold. I say 'fuck', and realise I've said it in a German accent, as if it were spelled 'fack'. My hands and toes have begun to thrum with numb pain from being out too long. I can't stop thinking that if I'd swum, I'd be warmer.

I bike slowly, so it takes me an hour to reach the train. Once on board, warmth rushes over me again. I take off my gloves and move my bony fingers, straining new life into their joints. And then, looking down, I see that my leg is covered in a deep and spreading red. Blood from the fall. It must have been frozen while I was outside, and now, in the warmth of the S-Bahn, is pooling into my clothes. I swing my foot on to the seat next to me, rolling up my leggings to reveal a cut as deep as my kneecap, warm and red, streaming across my leg. I stare at it blankly. A woman sitting across from me winces.

It's been a failure. That's what my mind calls the whole day, almost automatically. I packed my bag the way I always do: towel, underwear, extra socks, plastic bag, hammer, hot water, lunch, thermos, bike-repair kit, first-aid kit. I dressed warmly. But I didn't swim. Something in the day – the ice, the skaters, the fall – frustrates me. There is something I've been prevented from feeling, an urge unanswered. I look at my kneecap again – the wound yellow under the skin – and the thought arrives that in all of this swimming, I'm not completely sure what I'm doing. Like I've been trying to force some feeling out, to shock it from my system in the ice. Like I've been picking at a wound, preventing it from scabbing over.

I spent the weeks after the Oxford Street accident in a sling, holding my separated shoulder in place, taking trips to London hospitals I'd never seen before, seeing doctors, and getting X-rays. I grew sick from painkillers, so the doctor prescribed stomach medication. Amy helped me into and out of my clothes, styled my hair, and reached for things in the kitchen cupboard. I guarded my shoulder beneath my winter coat, terrified of being bumped into on the Tube.

I hadn't expected to resist the city, but those weeks were shrouded in my own shame at needing help, at being injured. Friends and doctors told me I was making progress, that a slump in mood was perfectly ordinary after physical trauma. But I couldn't ride my bike or swim or do normal things for myself, and resentment welled in the creases of my days. I had begun to sink into something uncontrolled, unwanted.

London had changed in my years away. I didn't remember it being so expensive, or needing to work quite so hard to get by. Places that had seemed alive and interesting some years earlier had begun to feel sterile and empty, despite the crowds. Restaurants that had been popular in 2008 had franchised and rolled out across the city. Friends had moved to the outskirts, looking for spare bedrooms and reasonable rents. The hospitals I visited were stark, the A&Es at risk of closure. I'd left before the cuts had hit deeply and returned to find things different than I remembered.

I worked a lot, throwing myself into the research I could do with just one hand. On weekends, I worked part-time as an events assistant, shuffling guests to their seats, checking on catering, minding my arm. At night, I spoke to Jacob. After the card and after the accident, his friendship became more vital than ever. I sent him pictures of me in my sling. He asked about my progress in healing. We talked about trips we could take together, camping trips in the West Country, bike rides across Northern Germany.

We talked side by side on our pillows, on FaceTime, and new, pervasive intimacy grew up between us, in the distance between Berlin and London, in the time we spent apart. The distance of the screen made it possible.

The months in Berlin had worked something into me, some idea or some longing, and the accident seemed to crystallise it. It was more than just him. I longed for Berlin. I began to dream of the cities overlaid on to one another, the Circle Line flowing into the Ringbahn, the creeping edges of London dissolving into Brandenburg countryside. I missed riding my bike across that flat landscape. I missed the forests and I missed the lakes.

There's a term glaciologists use for the rocks that are picked up and moved around by glaciers. 'Glacial erratics', they call them, from the Latin *errare:* to wander, to roam, to be mistaken, to go astray. Erratics carry their origins with them, telling the story of where a glacier has been and how the ice deposited the erratic in the landscape. An erratic is a rock that doesn't belong to the geology in which it is planted; instead, it's a record of another place. They appear wherever glaciers have been. They're in Ontario, near my family's cottage, and in Nova Scotia, shaping the coast-line. They're in Brandenburg, a geological record of the ice, like the lakes. Fontane writes of erratics in the first pages of *Der Stechlin*; they are part of the geology of the place. Like an erratic, I was carrying past places with me. I felt mistaken.

For the first time, I felt adrift in London, like I wasn't where I was meant to be. This place I'd sought out, the home I thought I was coming back to had disappeared. I wasn't sure if the accident had knocked it out of me or if it hadn't been there all along.

firn

Stolzenhagener See is capped with mist. Thin ice greases its edges, slick with meltwater and grey. Damp has reached under my skin into my bones, so I'm walking ever faster to warm up. If I trace the western edge of the lake, I'll find a spot to swim.

On the train up, the heating had been on full and I'd had the illusion of summer: green grass out the window, deer grazing in field after field. But then snow had appeared in patches, stitching the edge of a field to a creek. A white crane stood by the creek, watching the water, hiding in plain sight.

The path here is wet from melting snow and forms sticky brown ridges wherever I step. The entire forest seems to be melting – the slick shine of the lake like a glassy eye. A drier, colder day would have been better, I think; the damp is the worst. I wonder if the winter will be short, will peter out in a spell of rain.

The trail is lined with holiday homes grown thick with

lichen. They each have little gates that lead out towards the lake, rusting in the wet air. It's a private lake, owned since the nineteenth century by one of Germany's wealthiest families: *Betreten verboten*, the signs all read. I walk to the northern tip of the lake, finding nothing. Fences line the entirety of this side of the lake, so I'll have to pick one of them to climb.

I back-track a way, swinging around the side of a tall wrought-iron gate that floats atop a dock – no fencing attached to it, and to climb past it you have to dangle over the lake – and sit down on the wet wood, pulling off my boots. The lake water looks brown in the shallows, filled with leaf and mud, before slipping out into an icy cap of grey.

I step out into the lake, the cold of it burning my feet, and launch myself forward. My breath comes heavily today – I'm anxious out here alone – and I count my strokes aloud. One to twenty-five, swimming out towards the ice, and then I turn back, counting the strokes of my return. I'm back at forty-six. A short swim, but it's enough. I haven't seen a single person today, and I'm cautious on my own in the ice.

The quiet of the lake here isn't peaceful: it feels vacated of tranquillity, a thick and melting isolation running off into the ground, and I find myself wanting company, even a stranger, a walker on the trail. But no one comes, just the hollow sound of a woodpecker working its way through the trees, so I slide out of the shallows and into my clothes again, making small jumps on the spot to warm myself up.

The temperature of January has fluctuated by the week,

ice melting and re-forming, cloudier each time. I've watched it change from clear to grey as the weeks have passed. At the lake, the damp cold still hangs heavily, but by the time I've walked the four kilometres back to the train station in Wandlitz, the sun has come out.

I have an hour's wait for the train, so I slip into the bakery by the station and order a coffee with a slice of cake. The yellow Formica of the bakery counter reminds me of summer. I don't think it has changed since reunification. I stop here often on my way to and from the lakes nearby, and each time it feels as if I've stepped into a prior decade, the synthetic decor of another time, this place a stark but small comfort. I sit perched on a plastic chair, stirring my coffee. Madonna's 'Holiday' comes on the bakery's fuzzy radio, and I feel warm again.

The cut on my knee has scabbed over and begun to form a deep, grey scar where I've picked at it. I've kept it bandaged when swimming, but run my fingertips over it each night, the grains of the wound sliding off into scar tissue. I can't stop touching it, the same way I close my eyes and run my fingers over my tattoos to check if I can feel the lines of them in my skin. The scar and the lines of ink are a kind of record of time passing and I want them to remain. There's a bump on my shoulder bone where there shouldn't be.

In my reading about ice, I learn about the snow that blankets temperate glaciers, old snow that melts and recrystallises until it has the texture of wet sugar. 'Firn', from the Middle High German *virne* – meaning 'old, last year's' – compacts over time, over years, eventually becoming ice. Until that point, though, it reshapes itself with the seasons, the residue of past times reconstituting itself in the cold present.

The melting and re-forming snow here in Berlin and Brandenburg will never do that; it only happens on glaciers in the mountains, or in the far north or the far south. But nonetheless as the winter carries on fluctuating I imagine it between my fingers, sticky and granular. The *Encyclopedia Arctica* says that when it reaches this stage, it doesn't melt any longer but compacts, eventually becoming a part of the glacier.

I think a lot about last winter, about the accident and about how I changed. About why I felt I had to start swimming alone. The anger with myself and the heartbreak have dissipated and turned into a dull, steady presence. My shoulder still aches when I wake up in the morning. It probably always will. In the past decade my mother's knuckles have grown thick with arthritis – worse when she works in the garden – and I wonder if my joints will do the same. I've developed the habit of sliding my right shoulder back every time I move, rotating the joint in hopes it won't ice over. There's no visible scar except this habitual movement, this overcorrection.

I'm on the top deck of the bus, feeling faint. I've been in bed for two days with norovirus, clinging to a metal mixing bowl, fevered and forehead glistening. It's my first day out again, having managed a slice of dry toast for breakfast, and I see that I've missed very little: the weather is still grey and damp. The snow has gone, but a thinning coat of ice still caps the lakes.

The bus drives west from Spandau, crossing the line of the Mauerweg and the border of Brandenburg, dropping me at the side of a busy road. I duck off into the residential streets, eventually finding the worn track that leads to Neuer See.

It's a small suburban lake in the middle of a park. A tiny beach near one end is littered with the blown-out scraps of fireworks, a sure sign of Berlin winter revealed by the melted snow. In Germany, fireworks are only sold and allowed to be set off at New Year, so they are lit in abundance, a deluge of light in the dark winter. They linger afterwards, wasting with the days.

A thin rain begins to fall as I follow the track around the southern edge of the lake, and by the time I reach the lake's western tip, it's falling heavily over the water and the trail. I pull my hood up tight and cross my arms for warmth. The rain is pooling on the remaining lake ice, giving everything a slick, oiled look. There's a playground ahead, so I take temporary shelter under a wooden pirate ship.

Once the heaviest rain passes, I half-heartedly begin to look for a spot to swim. The large, curling shape of Falkenhagener See hugs closely to Neuer See, the larger left by glaciers, the smaller by a sand pit. The lakes are two records in the landscape. A small path runs between them, and I follow it a while, looking for a clearing. The best one is occupied, a sou'westered fisherman perched on a stool, despite the drizzle. I don't want to disturb him, so I carry on until I find another small opening in the trees, then slip myself through towards the water.

Avoiding bottle caps and shards of glass, I step out into

the sand. The water feels warmer today than it has in weeks – though I know it is still no warmer than three or four degrees – so I stand a while in the rain before swimming out into the lake's centre, where the waves settle into a glassy stillness near the ice. I swim towards the ice. Now softened and pitted with the warmth of the rain, it has the texture of slush, and comes apart in my hands. It's only slightly colder than the water; the sensation of it melts away as I touch it.

The following week, I go for lunch with Luca and Baptiste from the studio. We're eating Italian food when Baptiste tells me a story of a man who couldn't feel pain. The man was subjected to studies, he tells me, in which scientists would slam a hammer down next to his hand. He wouldn't flinch. The sensations we all learn to avoid, the painful experiences we gather and begin to understand as harmful, didn't make sense to the man.

I'm midway through a lasagne when Baptiste begins speaking, and when he finishes, I realise I've been holding my fork aloft, rapt in attention. I don't and could never understand the reality of such a condition, but something about this man sounds so familiar. Things that ought to have hurt didn't register.

When the body enters cold water – like any physical trauma – it responds. 'Cold shock response' is the body's reaction to the drop in temperature, the pain of the water. Because water conducts heat better than the air, the shock of the cold is far greater in a freezing lake than simply being out on a cold day. The water draws the warmth out of the body faster.

The initial response is a gasp, which can be the biggest risk in cold-water swimming. Gasping, you risk breathing in water and drowning. It's why I won't let first-time winter swimmers jump in to the water. Tachycardia sets in: the heart races. The body urges you out. The key is to keep moving. Entering the water slowly, step by step, it's possible to steady the breath. It's possible to feel the pain of the water strike and then dissipate. By mid-winter, once I've acclimatised, I hardly react at all.

There's a popular misunderstanding about hypothermia. People ask if I worry about freezing to death when I swim. I explain that it would take at least half an hour or more for hypothermia to set in, and by then I'm out and dry and rapturous. Two to three minutes in a frozen lake can suffice. I stay in long enough to move from pain to pleasure, counting my strokes.

Water under eleven degrees is considered 'cold' by scientific standards: it's enough to induce cold shock response, to drastically impair your muscle functions. Shivering is a common response at first. It sets in quickly at the beginning of the season. It's the body's effort to produce heat. But repeatedly exposing the body to the cold changes things: the water doesn't seem so bad after a few weeks. You come to expect it. There's no shock, but rather a stillness, an ability to observe the sensation of ice on the body. As the weeks pass and my body comes to expect the cold, the quaking takes longer to arrive. I don't shiver until long after I've left the water. Instead, I'm attuned to the sensation. The more subtle variations between temperatures become apparent: the cold of the sea in winter is milder than the ice of the lakes. Some lakes – Weißer

See, for example – hold the cold better than others, such that a five-degree swim at one lake is easily differentiated from a one-degree swim in another.

The joy of it is the body's response to pain. The cold triggers an endorphin release that diminishes the discomfort of swimming, blocking pain and producing euphoria. I've met opiate users who liken the sensation of cold-water swimming to using heroin. Perhaps they exaggerate, but I return to it again and again, looking for the high.

Baptiste is still talking about the painless man. I've eaten my lunch, but the entire time I've been absent, thinking about the water, about the cold and the ice. A crack forms, like the small, white split that appears as I hammer into the ice. My thoughts turn to Jacob, and then to my husband, both present and then absent again, these inconsistent figures in my memory. The sorrow is scarred over but ever present.

I think of what the lakes meant to me then and what they mean to me now. In the middle of the lake, I'm completely present. I'm no longer afraid to be alone. I've conditioned myself to the lake, to the cold, to the pain of it. I can hold it. I've made it mine.

out of air

When I had just about healed from the taxi accident, I took a train to Scotland for a few days of research in a private archive in Dundee. It was February by then, and the winter had laid itself thickly over England. As I rode the night train north it quickly became apparent that the train's heating was broken. The carriage filled with frozen air, and as I pressed my face up against the glass, I saw snow beginning to fall in the dark. The train felt cold, metallic, like a flashlight cutting through a black night.

I was travelling alone, hoping to immerse myself in work at the archives. But I spent the journey with Jacob at the other end of the internet, messaging all the while. Wind rushed through from the doors of the adjoining carriage, so I tucked myself into my coat, clutching my phone to me. Sleep came only in glimpses, snatches of quiet solitude in the cold until we reached Edinburgh and they repaired the heating. Then it was just a couple more hours until Dundee, and I slept fully.

In the morning, I pressed my head against the window and peered through the dark: the middling slate-blue of morning was beginning to stretch its breath across the landscape. We crossed the Tay and crawled into the city, still street-lit and silent. From there I took a bus. The archive wouldn't be open until nine, so I had decided to swim. It was one of my first swims since the accident. The bus led me north, along the coast, until the stone buildings of the city crept ever lower, and I found myself in a quiet stretch of a former fishing village, Broughty Ferry.

I had read that the local outdoor swimming club – Ye Amphibious Ancient Bathing Association – swam here, but I had been too shy to reach out. My shoulder was only just beginning to move again, and I was dipping into water only tentatively. I hadn't swum properly in over a month.

I followed a quiet waterfront path around Broughty Castle and along the beach on the Firth of Tay. Light was beginning to touch the horizon, pink and gold on the water. I undressed on the beach and piled my clothes neatly near the waterline. The sand was cool, cream-soft beneath my feet. The cold night on the train had gone from my limbs, but I wanted the water as much to wake me up as to free me from the journey.

I stepped out up to my waist and then swam, delicately, paddling one-armed, watching the sun lift itself into my sight-line. I'd never been to Scotland before and I'd never swum in the North Sea. I stayed in the shallows, floated in that interstitial space between river and sea, tucked safely at the edge of the landscape.

The sun was reaching above the horizon, so I clambered

back to shore and dressed slowly in the last dregs of the darkness, watching as the sky burned red and orange. There was no wind. I was alone. In the stillness of the morning, I wanted Jacob there with me.

Impetuously, impulsively, I booked a ticket to Berlin. I hoped that seeing him might give form to this amorphous feeling I'd been holding. I'd hoped to catalyse a change between us. By the end of the week I was stepping carefully down a creaking aircraft stairwell. Jacob met me at Arrivals, held me close a moment, inspected my bad shoulder, and then turned and led me to the train. Not home, but south: so we could swim.

Zeesener See sat a few kilometres south of Königs Wusterhausen, at the end of a marshy wetland. It was a long, thin lake, marine blue and capped with ice. Clear white snow lined the ground and coated the ice, the fingertips of wind touching the blue of the water. Midway along the lake we found a dock and decided to swim.

It was cold – winter was still holding fast on to February. We undressed quickly, stripping down to our skin in the tight cold, looking properly at one another for the first time. The furtiveness of the previous autumn was gone. A small ladder dipped down into the lake, and he watched me climb down into the blue. He followed me down, the glacial rush of water swelling between our legs, over our chests, and around our necks. The sensation of cold didn't surprise me, but it stopped my breath momentarily, powerfully, with the rolling force of an ocean rushing on to shore. It was our last new lake together.

When we'd first met, there had been a glint of recognition: a feeling of sameness, of understanding. I felt that he could push me to grow in ways that I couldn't quite grasp. In the months we spent together, swimming, I became someone else. Someone stronger and braver. I didn't know if I could be that person without him. I'd longed to give shape to our love, but it was impossible. He was present and then absent again, retreating as he had months before. Immediately, I regretted the visit, felt that I'd somehow catalysed an ending. On the last day, I stood in his doorway, ready to go, heartbroken.

When I'd been on the train to Scotland, I had sent him a picture of the carriage and he'd said of the seat across from me, 'That's my seat.' And it was. He had been there the whole ride, he always was, at the other end of the internet, at the other end of the phone. But now, standing directly in front of me, an arm's distance away, he wasn't here. He was capable of putting an ocean between us with a word, with a glance. A gap opened up wider than the distance between countries, between matter and text message words, and he raised his hand as if in salute, saying only, 'Thanks for coming.'

It's February, a year after Scotland and that visit to Berlin. I'm thirty-six lakes into my year of swimming. I'm up early. The sun sits just above the bare skeletons of the trees, which are coated in hoar-frost. A thin armour of white cold covers everything. The streets are silent but for the birds: the songs of blackbirds and great tits swell in the air, landing on the stillness of everything else. I don't see a single person the entire way to the lake.

I've come back to Zeesener See now, alone, as if to exorcise a ghost. I want to swim here again, to see if anything of what I remember is right, if it really was as blue as I had thought it had been. More than anything, I want to forget him. I want the cold of the lake to anaesthetise the remaining hurt and anger, to wash it off of me, if it can.

The lake sits on the eastern side of the village of Zeesen, a small residential stretch outside Königs Wusterhausen. I've been here a number of times on my way to other lakes, and have come to know its streets. It's the kind of quiet place where chickens stray from their yards, roaming the lanes confidently. Locals advertise household services like ironing and childcare from their front windows. Children ride their bikes up and down the roads. An enormous abandoned manor house sits crumbling near the village's centre. To me, the house looks like sadness.

I take Schulstraße towards the lake, following the intermittent paving stones along the road. It's nine in the morning and Zeesen is silent: no dog walkers or cyclists. It feels, in a way, as if the town had frozen overnight with the weather, empty, in a suspended state. The sun edges higher in the clear sky, and still there's only the sound of bird song. Ahead of me, I see a collared dove standing in a driveway. It sees me too and turns away. The birds have better things to do.

I reach the lake through a small metal gate and make my way towards the dock. It's exactly as I remember it: the bluest lake and the bluest sky, and the long wooden dock stretching out into the water. There are ducks and cormorants floating nearby in the only fluid patch of water. The rest is glazed with a thin, rippling ice that moves with the waves. It must have formed overnight as the rest of the town fell silent.

I stand a while on the edge of the dock, watching the birds fly. They settle fifty yards northwards, near but not too close. They're the only ones here with me. Ahead of me, the lake opens up, an undulating stretch of curves edging towards the horizon, white with morning sun. The distant end of Zeesener See is cast in air frost, rising in the light the way smoke rises from dry ice. I realise now how cold it is.

The longer I stand here, the closer to the surface my thoughts rise, and I don't want to hold them today. It's so beautiful out and I want to linger in it, to feel the sun and the cold and the blue fully on my skin. I undress and place my clothes neatly atop my bag, stepping from my boots on to the wet wood of the dock. It is slick with bird shit.

I step towards the ladder and lower myself down rung by rung into the cold. There's ice on the other side of the dock and as I settle into the deep water, waves roll under its surface, making the entire lake creak and roll rhythmically. It makes small cracking sounds in the silence. The intensity of that day here last year is gone: instead, I swim slowly, silently, watching the ice. My heart aches, but only distantly. I feel the lake on me, around me. The water feels thin, clean, and as I move through it I feel it ripple down my limbs and across my back. There is life in the cold.

I climb back up the ladder and watch the entire lake move: fluidly, adaptably. The ice doesn't break up, but creaks and settles with the water, dancing at the surface. I want to be like the ice, but it's warm up here in the air. I'm not of the lake, not of the ice. The sun is warming the water from my skin, and soon I will be dry. I watch the droplets bead on my arms and then disappear into the dry cold of the day.

It isn't what I thought it would be. I don't know what I had expected. But a stillness, a silence hangs over it all, asking me to acknowledge it. I'd come for an exorcism, to wash myself of pain and grief, but instead I find silence. I feel the ghost settle into my body, into my skin, and into the air. The ache in my heart doesn't go. It stays with me, like the ice on the lake, as if to say, 'I'm here, moving with you.'

echo

The wintry cold has dissipated and the ice has gone. The first weeks of February are bright, the air warming and the sun gleaming behind a pattern of white cloud. I've been working the past weeks with a kind of focused, microscopic attention, editing chapters of my dissertation that I've read again and again, nearing a final draft. But I've managed to save the weekends for swimming. Still, though, I'm late, cycling furiously through Mitte to reach the train in time. I dodge pedestrians as I take the corner at Friedrichstraße, pushing my way up towards the station. My phone is buzzing in my pocket; Anne is waiting.

I heave my bike up the stairs and find her on the platform. The train is pulling in. She's got the tickets already – Anne is as keen on plans and preparation as I am – and as I catch my breath, she is unflustered. We wheel our bikes into the carriage and then turn, at last, to greet one another good morning.

The train cuts diagonally across the city, down towards

Potsdam, stopping at Babelsberg. The district – famous for its film studio, the first major studio in the world – sits east of central Potsdam, and from here we cycle further east, towards Güterfelde. As we cycle, Anne tells me about her family. She carries a mint-green tote bag with two sausages on it, curving around the words *Wurst Freund*. I laugh at this – bending the words into their English sounds – because she is beginning to be my best friend here. But Anne explains that it is her family's old business, a butcher's shop. She loves the logo, she tells me, and only has two of these bags. She says this simply, unsentimentally, which, now that I know her, betrays its importance.

Our plan is to swim in Güterfelder Haussee, a reed-lined lake hidden quietly amidst the fields and motorways south of Berlin. It's a lake outshone by the bigger, bluer lakes near Potsdam: few but the locals seem to know about it, and when we arrive, there are just a few dog walkers leaving the forest.

I had texted Anne the day before with the route, and she'd written back asking if I had understood the significance of the lake's name. I'd admitted that I hadn't – I have yet to inhabit German in the way I do English, drawing lines between words and their associations, their hidden selves – so she explained. Güterfelde, she told me, was not the village's original name. She sent me a link to a local news article: the village had celebrated its seven-hundred-and-fifty-year jubilee a few years before, and a local had taken up a campaign to change the name of the town back to its original name: Gütergotz. The name – of Slavic origin – was just one of many place names that had been Germanised under the Nazis in the late 1930s. Originally meaning 'morning guest' – or in some cases translated as 'morning god' – it was changed, removing the 'gotz' and replacing it with the more German-sounding 'feld', meaning 'field'. It was one of the many ways in which German identity was manufactured, constructed and delimited. In Brandenburg, the tension between Slavic and German names is a constant; in most cases, the two origins overlap, and have grown together over time.

The lake's name, Güterfelder Haussee, Anne explained, was analogous to the common German term *Hausberg*, denoting a town's mountain or hillside. In this flat landscape, not a hill or mountain in sight, Güterfelde has its lake. As the season carries on, Anne will point out these words from time to time: words that sound Slavic, words that sound German, words that carry histories within them. It is one of the ways she teaches me about landscape, about Germany.

We follow the trail into the woods, dodging the dog walkers. Anne hates dogs and spends the walk looking for their tracks on the lake-shore, making sure we don't inadvertently swim from a dog beach. I laugh at her and wander ahead through the woods. The winter has done its work: chickweed has spread thickly across the forest floor, a winter carpet for the trees. The wood is a mixture of beech and oak, and common ivy grows over all of it, a thick blanket of dark green in the brown, dark berries dangling from the choking clusters. Anne looks up at them, having forgotten about the dogs.

'It's like the trees are wearing dresses,' she says. I nod in agreement, wondering why she isn't always with me, teaching new words, sharing her thoughts. I'm suddenly so grateful for her presence, for someone so willing to plough into frozen water with me. For friendship rather than romance, the lack of complication in it.

We settle on a small reed-lined clearing and undress, stepping out into the cold. It's colder here than I expected – the sun can be deceiving – and I reel with pain as I wade up to my waist. But I move steadily forward. Anne follows, and we both swim out, taking in the length of the lake. It's sheltered and quiet, with a few cottages opposite us.

I stumble back to shore and, as I dry off, I notice a light figure on the opposite shore.

'He's swimming!' I say, and Anne turns, excitement rushing over both of us at the thought of a fellow swimmer. He's climbing out by now, drying off on the beach, and we're waving. He doesn't notice us, though, two hundred metres away, across the water. I get it, in a way, the tunnel vision that comes over you in the winter. In summer I can languish at the water's surface, taking in the world. In winter, my focus is acute, piercing. I feel only my hands, my feet.

The man wanders off, but Anne and I are curious now: the beach on the other side of the lake looks even nicer, so we pack up our things and follow the trail around. By the time we reach it, the cloud has cleared and left the sky bright and blue. It feels momentarily like spring, so we venture out on to the small dock that edges the beach and settle for lunch.

I unpack my sandwiches and boiled eggs – 'honest food', Anne calls it – and she takes out a packet of chocolate biscuits. We sit eating and drinking warm coffee, indulging in the sun, until I wonder if we ought to make the best of the weather and swim once more. Winter may be over soon, or this may just be a temporary lull. Anne agrees. We pack away our lunches and strip off our clothes again, this time taking turns, stepping down the ladder into the cold rung by rung, naked in the bright sun.

The water feels warmer the second time around – deceptively so – and I swim out fifty feet, turning on my back and letting the warm light wash over me. Floating at the surface, the break between air and water is the coolest part. Underneath, my limbs feel fluid and at home, the lake sliding over my skin, naked and alive.

The next morning is equally as bright, a small window of sunshine after January's weeks of grey. Anne and I have been so overjoyed after our visit to Güterfelder Haussee that we've decided to swim again. Nowhere new, but at Orankesee, where Anne has been swimming on Sundays with the local FKK swimming club, the Berliner Seehunde. The group has been swimming here since 1980, gathering weekly on the beach to swim nude during the winter months. I've not been before, but Anne has been joining them – mostly swimmers much older than us both – and I've decided to tag along.

The group has its benefits. They carve great swathes into the lake ice when it freezes over, making sure there's always room for a dip. They gather for celebrations together, for food and for friendship by the water. It is one of the ways in which local community has carried on despite the changes wrought in the country more widely.

Today, the sun gleams off the surface of Orankesee. The

swimmers are gathered on the sand, wearing red jackets and bathrobes embroidered with the club's name. The group's jolly membership co-ordinator Dieter wanders over in his bathrobe and greets me, recognising a new face. He shakes my hand and welcomes me in German, and Anne explains that I'm also a winter swimmer. He looks at me knowingly, remarks that we're both well-prepared for the cold then, and wishes us a good swim.

With that, the group strips off and rushes into the lake. Anne and I undress and then swim out into the water twice, the clear cold sharper than the day before. I stay in until the feeling in my fingers goes, and then retreat to shore, dress in the sunshine, and open my thermos.

Dieter comes back over to ask if I will join the group. It would be nice, I think, not to have to carry a hammer, to have the lake ready. The community would be a blessing, but I know that for now I want to carry on alone, as if I'm not quite finished proving my point. I hesitate, and then explain. But I tell him that I'll join next season, and I mean it, the thought of a future here flickering across my mind, across the surface of the lake.

unfolded

It starts to rain as soon as I hit the cobbled streets in the centre of Bernau. I've been here before – during that thunder-storm in late summer – and as I cycle north, I make a mental check-list of the streets and buildings I recognise. The city's defensive wall, built in the fifteenth century, forms a horseshoe around which the centre pivots, cobbled streets clustered within its enclosure. Timber-framed houses and *Plattenbau* – prefabricated housing rolled across the town's centre during the 1970s in an effort to establish Bernau as the ideal communist town – peter out quickly, and as I pass the red brick of St Marien Kirche and cut across the park, drenched green, I find myself on the open road leading north.

A cold wind rushes across the open country, heavy rain lashing my cheeks. I pull the hood of my jacket tighter and then pedal faster in hopes of finding a more sheltered road ahead. I'm on my way to Hellsee, a large lake ten kilo-metres north of Bernau, following a road that cuts across flat farmland before narrowing to one lane. It's freshly tarmacked and slick in the rain, and I feel increasingly precarious on my bike as cars speed past in the narrow space. Rain runs in heavy streams off my hood, and my hands are beginning to ache with damp cold. I'm not nearly halfway there.

The road passes an animal kennel – on the site of a former East German army bunker – and reaches a residential stretch, then forks off, up towards a thick patch of pine forest. At the trees' edge, the asphalt abruptly ends and becomes sand track. When I'd biked this stretch in summer, the rain had fallen so heavily that I'd had to dismount and wait out the storm with another woman under a bus shelter. I'd been given a new lake that day: Mechesee, a small, enclosed lake in the middle of the village of Lobetal. Now, reaching the edge of the forest, I slip off my bike and make a mental note of where I am: to my right, a small lake ripples under the falling rain. I know it instantly, without the map and without having ever been here before. It's Mechesee.

I think about the woman under the bus shelter – about her flowered dress and the small gift of a lake she'd given me that day in the rain. I wonder, momentarily, if the lake, like Bernau, exists only in the rain. I don't stop, though. I push my bike on to the sand track: I cycled this far to go to Hellsee.

The trail leads further north, past a water-treatment plant and on towards a thicker forest. The thick dampness of the air gives way to the smell of pine, and it briefly seems as though the weather might lift. But I walk further in, a kilometre into the woods, until I am overwhelmed by the thick odour of manure. I look around: there are only hunting blinds in this part of the woods, but the smell permeates everything. I take a turn around a treed corner, and there stand two hunters, clad in fatigues and armed, occupying the middle of the trail. I stop, vulnerability washing quickly across my mind, and then greet them. They pass me indifferently, saying nothing.

I glance at my map and see that I'm still four kilometres away from Hellsee. I think about Mechesee, back there in the village, enclosed by trees and patterned with rain. It looked sheltered, safe. I'd come across it today for a reason, I think, and for once, I relent. I turn back through the woods and am back in the village, rounding the western side of the lake. Hellsee can wait.

The middle of Mechesee is burnished flat – a shallow sand-bank at the lake's centre disrupting the rippled grey of the rain – and its edges are lined with reeds. I follow the path around the lake's tip, making for a small beach opposite. Late winter is dragging over the day, cladding the forest in an exhausted, damp mist. Between the trees, what look like small stumps appear, and then I realise they are graves – soldiers' graves – forgotten, spectral and sparsely lined through the forest. For a moment I walk towards them, and then pause, thinking better of it, back-tracking towards the lake. Lobetal, I'll learn later, has a number of army and naval bunkers, a town hiding so much underground, folded into the forests. One of the bunkers sits just beyond where I'd met the hunters in the woods. I glance out at the spot where the lake is glazed and still, the sand-bank underneath, hidden but ever present.

I find a small beach on the northern tip of the lake and

undress near a large oak tree. I neatly pile my clothes on my bike seat, covering them from the rain with my jacket, and then step towards the lake. It's not too cold – I've been out long enough that the cut of the cold has deadened – and the water is thin and opaque. I swim out, counting my strokes, and turn back to shore, thinking about the gift of the lake on a grim day. I step sodden and numb on to the sand. Just then, a woman with a large German shepherd appears on the path.

'*Waren Sie baden?*' she asks. I've come to expect this question. She looks horrified and amused all at once, so I begin to explain that the water's really quite fine. She eyes me suspiciously, chin raised, and then laughs and wanders off.

After that visit to Jacob, I went back to London and threw myself wholly into work. My doctorate became more consuming than ever before. I could work five days a week on research and weekends at my part-time job. The moments at work were a salvation: hours spent in archives, leafing through decaying legal files and land surveys. They held entire worlds in which to lose myself, to vacate my own feelings. Twice I found myself ushered out of archives at closing time, having worked eight hours straight without looking up, without food, water or a toilet break. My body deadened. The skin on my fingers cracked like the parchments I was reading.

In truth, part of me was switching off. Eight weeks after the accident the doctor diagnosed me with depression, pointing out that it was completely to be expected. Hormones react to shock, to impact. The concurrence of the accident with losing Jacob felt something of an inevitability, like I should have known it would happen, but still, I was surprised. I thought about the haunted look on my mother's face when I was a teenager and felt the weight of an unwanted inheritance settling upon me. I thought it was something I could work to avoid, like diabetes or heart disease, as if my own strength of will could keep the night from coming. I called Mom and asked how it had felt, and her words gave shape to my own vacancy of feeling. If I'd been capable of feeling fear, devastation, I would have.

I felt as though I'd been hung and dried on a precarious line – brittle, delicate, hollow. As a child, my grandmother had kept a vase of dried cat-tails in her living room. I touched one once, when I was six, and it scattered into nothing, leaving itself dissected in clouds on the carpet.

I cried only on the Tube platform – and only for the seconds it took for the train to rush in at Shepherd's Bush Market. The rest of the time I stood safely back from myself, pressing work into the vacated space that had once held feeling. When the doctor handed me a pamphlet and a prescription for Sertraline, I looked at the infographics and thought, distantly, that I'd never been more productive. I went home and threw the prescription away.

I could feel only one pleasure through it all. I was undertaking fieldwork for my doctorate, swimming with and interviewing the winter swimmers on the Heath, a kind of mandated cold-water therapy. I'd returned to the Ladies' Pond and found some sense of relief, as I had some years earlier. So as I curled inwards into bursts of work and catatonic sleep, the Heath opened itself up to me again. I swam in the cold three times a week and lost myself in the stories of the women there: their decades swimming through winter, free of men, free of intrusion. I found small moments of solace in those swims, moments of cut-glass clarity and feeling that I couldn't seem to summon at any other time, as if warmth was only to be found in the cold of the water.

I watched spring unfold on the Heath, blossom erupting, the catkins coming in, and the grip of the thing lightened. But I still worked with a sort of exhausted determination, wanting to finish the essential core of my research. I sensed – having never quite made the decision explicitly – that I wouldn't stay in London this time. As hard as I was working, my bank balance dwindled to zero every month. My scholarship was paid in Canadian dollars, and as the dollar dropped against the pound, I realised I was trying to force something into shape, to fit myself into a life I thought I ought to have, contorted and unhappy. The hold that Berlin had held on me months earlier hadn't waned.

The months at the Ladies' Pond felt like a kind of reclamation, the water a kind of reminder that I'd once found solace in swimming, that it wasn't simply something held between Jacob and me. It had once been mine – in the black of night at Chocolate Lake, in those early days at Krumme Lanke – and I could find that again, if I swam enough. If I returned to Berlin, I could write myself on to the landscape, on to my own memories of the place. I could layer new meaning on to the lakes. I could outrun depression. So I took the decision, left the life I thought I'd wanted in London, moved into the stark rented room in Prenzlauer Berg, and set out to the lakes.

*

The train station at Potsdam outlets on to a disorienting web of roads: concrete and traffic lights in multiple directions, no landmarks, no invitation. I've been here many times before, but each time have taken the wrong exit from the station, ended up wheeling my bike through the unnavigable crowds queuing for baguettes or train tickets. Anne and I take the wrong exit, then turn back up the stairs with our bikes hooked over our shoulders. She is eating a banana with one hand, her bike clutched in the other, swerving through the Saturday morning crowd, refusing to let me carry her bag.

We make it on to the road, finding our way from Friedrich-Engels-Straße to Leipziger Straße, towards Schwielowsee. The roads in Potsdam aren't built for cyclists, and we jostle for space in the thin margin of the gravel near the road's edge. Soon enough, though, the sparse concrete of the city ends and we are careening downhill into a forest-lined road alongside Templiner See. Winter has fallen away, the steady unfolding of early spring announced by a water-thin blue, cloudless sky. The trees are still bare, but new shoots of grass cluster in the lawns at the roads' edges. The scrubby margins of the wood reveal flashes of light reflected from the water as we cycle past.

The journey is quiet, so we bike side by side, laughing over stories of bad dates. Anne knows the route. She used to cycle it when she was married. Separation is one of the small threads that connects us. We are both in the process of rewriting memories. She watches for the road to Caputh, a small, cobble-streeted village on the edge of Schwielowsee. It's a quiet place in February, sun shining in wide angles across the lanes. A sign points the direction to Einsteinhaus, the scientist's holiday home – his only surviving residence in Germany – a rust-red house on the hill, overlooking the town and the lake. We follow the lane downhill, towards the water's edge, where the wide windows of a waterfront restaurant – Fährhaus Caputh – overlook the ferry landing. Anne stops us here, setting our intention for the day.

'This is where we'll cycle back to.' She points to a small, flat ferry boat shuttling a hundred yards between spits of land, joining the western shore with the eastern, through the confluence of Templiner See and Schwielowsee, the watery path of the Havel River. After that, she promises we'll return to the restaurant to have *Kaffee und Kuchen*, coffee and cake, a sweet promise after a day's cycling.

She leads southward down the lane, winding up a small hill that takes us away from the lake, up a quiet road that guides us out of the village. The road narrows and is edged by old brick walls, and then slopes downhill again into a sparse wood. The pines here are notched with slashes, deep Vs cut into the bark to extract pine resin for turpentine. The cuts – called streaks or cat faces – form a pattern, giving the practice its name: 'the Herringbone method'. Now widely discouraged, though it carries on, streaking the pines was until the mid-twentieth century a crucial part of the forest economy in a landscape dominated by pines. I step off my bike to look at the notches and as I begin to explain them, Anne stops me, gasping at the view. The hill opens up on to a steep slope, unfolding down towards Schwielowsee, which is pale blue in the light.

We wheel our bikes downhill along a dirt trail, and then

cycle further until we've reached the lawned gardens of Schlosspark Petzow. The landscaped gardens of the manor house were designed by Peter Joseph Lenné, Prussia's most famous landscape designer. During his time as head gardener in Potsdam, he created the extensive gardens at Sanssouci, the palace in Potsdam, and at the Pfaueninsel, the 'Peacock Island', which sits in the Havel. Lenné refined the natural style in German gardening, introducing the informal and picturesque sight-lines that have more often come to characterise English gardens. But Petzow's gardens are rather more modest, with just a few walks and a pond. As we wheel our bikes along the gravel path we pass a bride and groom posing for photographers against the early spring green.

We follow the trail towards the water's edge and find a small beach. Two women wrapped in fleece scarves and quilted coats sit on a blue bench overlooking the water, and as I undress down to a small bikini and step out into the lake, they remark to Anne that I could have just swum naked, they wouldn't have minded. I swim out into the lake as Anne chats to them. I can hear them talking about me but the farther out I swim the more distant their voices become, the more I feel only the sensation of cold water on my skin, sun at my forehead, a bright glistening on the lake's surface.

I turn back as Anne steps into the water, and I watch her descend into the crystal clear of it. The women on the bench are packing up to leave, and as they wander away I cry '*Tschüß*' from the water and they turn, waving at me, gesturing their encouragement. I swim back to shore, as if a part of me wants to go with them.

Back on the sand, a bracing rush ripples over my skin. I dry quickly in the sun, but the clarity of the cold remains, and I can feel it in my bones. I stayed in too long, the warmth of the day deceiving me somewhat. I dress quickly now, fumbling for the clothes strewn atop my bicycle's handlebars. Anne comes back to shore too and we move over to the bench. We sit for a while watching the water. I eat boiled eggs and drink coffee while Anne eats fondant egg sweets and drinks Earl Grey. There is an orange sticker on the bench, peeled from the cover of someone's book. It reads only, *Nobelpreis für Literatur 2014*, and Anne begins listing authors, searching herself for the year's winner. She grows frustrated, takes a picture of the sticker, and files the thought away for a later time. Later in the evening, I'll receive a text reading only: Patrick Modiano!

When we're finished, we pack our bags and cycle back to the path, finding our way northward around the western shore of the lake. It leads us past a sea-buckthorn plantation and up through a series of new waterside developments. Anne looks dismayed at the sight of them, boxes on the waterfront, closing ranks around the lake. I try to imagine them elsewhere and my mind lands in a suburban plot in south-east England, then a development in south-western Ontario. Their grey and white stucco cuts through the green, through the blue of the lake, like air-dropped containers. These houses are too anonymous for this place.

We round the top of the lake where the land thins between Templiner See and Schwielowsee, approaching the ferry back to Caputh. Anne wants to swim once more, gesturing towards an open stretch beyond a campsite near the boats in Templiner See. I'm still cold and can't bear the thought of stripping back down to bare skin, so I zip my jacket up to my chin as I watch her dip in to the water's edge. She swims out steadily through a patch of shadow, stretching her arms out into the sunlight ahead of her. She swims with the kind of tenacity that belongs to winter swimmers, getting in the water when no one else would. I look at the lake, muddy and leaf-strewn here, and watch her with fascination, with respect. She's stronger than I am.

We cycle on to the ferry, a flat-iron boat with room for two cars and a few bikes, shuttling the short distance between the shores. The boatman collects our fare and launches us across, back to Fährhaus Caputh. It's busy out now, crowds lining the waterfront in late afternoon, but we manage to find a small booth in the glassed-in sun terrace of the restaurant.

Anne orders us a plum cake and cream so large we struggled to finish it between us. We sit watching the other diners, an old couple next to us eating potatoes and sausages. The old man chats to Anne in German for a while, talking about the spring-time, about the return of the sun, and about the size of our slice of cake. He turns to me occasionally and translates into an American-inflected English, which makes me smile, as he doesn't realise I am following the conversation, albeit silently. His wife smiles quietly too, saying nothing.

We bike back to Potsdam side by side, taking the quiet road out of Caputh. I turn to Anne to tell her how much I've loved the day, and she pauses in reply, searching for words.

'I don't know how to explain this,' she begins, 'but swimming like this has meant so much to me. It's as if it opened something in me, like a drawer or something folded, what's the word, one of those files,'

'An accordion file,' I offer.

'Yes, there's more space inside than it originally seemed.'

I cycle on, thinking about this, about what her friendship has come to mean to me. I think about Anne's second swim, the strength I'd seen in her pushing through the cold. Swimming seemed to give strength a form, to give materiality to reserves held inside.

I've been so angry with myself for losing my equilibrium, for confusing swimming with love. I've been furious at myself for sinking, for being vulnerable to periods of depression that were prefigured inside me. But Anne is right. There is more space inside than I can imagine, more hope and possibility than I'd known. Feeling as clear as the day, as deep as the lake.

borderland

From the Barents Sea, north of Finland and Russia, to the Adriatic and Black Seas, running from the top of Europe to the south, there is a stretch of land that has remained relatively undisturbed since the middle of the twentieth century. During the Cold War, this was the border, the so-called Iron Curtain. Today, it makes up the conservation land known as the European Green Belt.

Not a single wall or a narrow border, the stretch between the two Germanys was as wide as a kilometre in places, 1,393 kilometres of borderland that remained active until reunification. Entire communities existed within these spaces – villages that, whether through political bartering or pure chance, ended up in the Sperrgebiet, 'prohibited area', along the border. These communities existed in a kind of vacuum – deeply patrolled and regulated, yet removed from the maps and road signs, to prevent escapees from finding the border. There are stories of the West-facing façades of village buildings being modernised and renovated, a Potemkin show put on for West Germans peering over the border with binoculars.

As those villages persisted and adapted to their newly liminal identities – despite fences, land mines, trip wires, patrol roads, watch towers and curfews – so too did nature take its course. Satellite imagery of the Finnish-Russian border in the seventies captured deep-green strips of old-growth forest, the first indication that within the untraversed stretch of the Cold War borderlands, the natural world had begun to thrive. By the 1980s, rare birds had appeared in the intra-German border, and today, preserved as a cross-cultural natural monument, the border remains a haven for moss, bats and other wildlife.

The borders within Berlin have been somewhat different. In the much narrower Todesstreifen, 'the death strip', efforts to make use of the land – once raked over with sand and gravel to reveal the footprints of escapees – have been less coherent. The Berliner Mauerweg, the trail established in the early 2000s, marks the route of the Wall – and the fences that formed the outer city border – encircling the former West Berlin. In the years since, efforts to make use of the now dormant space left by the death strip have flickered, proposals for landscaped gardens and recreational areas leading to little. Within the inner city, memorials have been erected and new construction advances into these empty stretches of land, but there are entire sections of the border that remain unmarked, forgotten. Berlin is like this – redevelopment faltering in the sand of memory – but it is changing. Condo blocks have sprung up where buildings have been laid waste. Glass boxes overlook the death strip.

I didn't know the location of the border the first time I came to Groß Glienicker See. I hadn't looked closely enough at the map of the GDR – West Berlin just a blank spot, an absence – and seen that the border cut the lake exactly in half. The lake ended in a sea of white paper. I hadn't known that instead of a wall, instead of a fence, there had been a floating border here: a net, a line of buoys, patrols by boat. On the West Berlin shore, on the beach I'm standing on now, there had stood a sign: *Achtung: In 170m endet West-Berlin*. The beach was the shore of a walled island.

That day I'd been unable to swim here, when the lake had been too frozen, is still weighing on me. I've not stopped thinking about the lake since, wanting to feel what was beneath the ice. It's the beginning of March, and while winter has gone for the most part, the weather remains cold and damp. The same grey wash that spread itself over the late autumn hangs over late winter, await-ing sun and warmth. They haven't arrived yet. I step towards the water, eyes to the sky, watching a cloud roll in. The ceiling is low today, a thick, looming grey, and as soon as I begin to undress, a light patter of rain rolls out over the lake. I'm alone here but for a group of divers packing up nearby, escaping the rain. They load their gear into a cluster of white vans and then stand, watching the weather.

I pile my clothes under my raincoat and step on to the wet sand. It's cold and sinks under the weight of my feet as I move across it, leaving tracks. The lake itself is a sheet, broken only by the pock marks of the rain, a grey extension of the sky above it. The far shore – which would have been the East – remains silent, no leaves on the trees, a putty-coloured stroke on the horizon. At Christmas in 1989, the border was opened between the villages of Groß Glienicke in the GDR and Kladow in West Berlin, allowing locals to go to church together for the first time since the Wall was erected. The day turned into such a celebration that the *Taggespiegel* reported that locals in the East decorated the gateway with Soviet military hats and brought a Trabant – one of the GDR's state-issued cars – to provide a bit of local colour. This fetish for the East has been rendered in German as *Ostalgie*, a portmanteau of 'east' and 'nostalgia', a material recognition that a way of life isn't easily dismantled and such a dismantling isn't universally desired. Artefacts remain, among other less tangible things.

Despite reunification, however, this lake still marks an invisible border. On the beach, I stand in Berlin. The other side of the lake is Brandenburg, the city-country border running through the water, now only a dotted line on a map. Negotiation is a constant.

The day I'd been here in winter – with the hockey players and the haunting yowling of their skates – I'd been transfixed by the place, despite the cold, despite the ice. Now, in the rain, the feeling hasn't dissipated: there is something about the lake, the clarity of the water, the way it sits silently, unassumingly, on the edge of the city, that has convinced me that I love it. I scan the horizon, looking for reasons or signs, but see only the thick reeds at the lake's edge – golden highlights on a dull brown background – and the grey of the water. There is nothing exceptional about the day or the place, but it holds itself stoically, a silent shore, and I have a kind of respect for it.

I swim out into the lake – tracing broad loops in the shallows – and watch the opposite shore. Near the north-western tip of the lake, there had been a guard station, a watch tower overlooking the border. The city's memorial website has a photo gallery of that stretch of the border. A slider moves between a still shot of the death strip and the growing young forest in its place, strips of bare sand and a sandy trail through the woods. At first the present-day view looks inviting, silent about its past. But the young trees – skinny birch, aspen, and ash trees – are a record, pioneer trees reclaiming bare ground. At Sacrower See, just south of here, I had seen rows of birch at the edge of the pathway – trunks peeling bright white – quietly colonising the ground of the death strip. Berlin and Brandenburg hold a lot of new forest.

My shoulders stiffen as I work my way out into the lake. Cold, bright drops of rain soak through my hat and into my hair, the late winter washing over me from every direction. I turn back towards the beach, treading water a moment, and feel the depth of the lake beneath me. Berliners swam here, despite the buoys, even then. An out-of-date internet forum maintained by GDR history-buffs details local memories of the lake: swimming in summer, the orange buoys, the mesh net, the unfortunate border-crossers who were picked up in the middle of the lake. They link to old photographs, to news articles and to old maps. Beyond these fragments, little remains of the aqueous border, the lake's memories held in hypertext.

The scuba-divers on the beach are lingering, and as I emerge back on the sand one of them walks over. He is tall, lumbering towards the shore, his brown hair matted by rain. He doesn't say anything, just gives me a puzzled look and then turns back to the lake, standing ten feet away, as if he wants to talk.

I open: '*Waren Sie tauchen?*' Were you diving?

He looks at me confused, as if he is surprised I'd noticed, and then explains that the weather today isn't great for diving. The water is normally very clear here – fantastic for spotting stocky, grey-finned tench, carp, perch and water plants on the lake's bottom – but today there is too much sediment. I look back out at the water, patterned with rain drops, and think about the depth of it beneath me when I'd been twenty metres out. I hadn't been able to see my feet.

I turn back to the man, but he's talking about diving in detail now, and my German can't keep up. I look at him confused and explain that I'm struggling to follow, but his explanations don't seem to help. We struggle, line for line, until we both smile and call it even. I wish him a good day, but I'm mortified, wishing my German was better. I am frustrated with myself for opening the conversation and then being unable to finish it. I run through the phrases I understood – about the clarity of the water, about the fish and the plants – and then begin to dress and pack up.

The day is dreary – the rain hasn't ceased – so I don't bother to eat my lunch. I pour out a steaming capful of coffee from my thermos, knock it back as I wheel my bike back towards the road. I think about the lake here in summer – the reeds turned to green, the water clear in the sun – and know I'll come back, always, the place already precious to me.

swell

There's a lake at the southern edge of the city – a wide, shallow pan, the biggest in Berlin. Shaped by glaciation and fed by the Spree River, Großer Müggelsee sits like a mouth agape, a culmination of flows, a testament to the city's long relationship with water. As early as the thirteenth century, Müggelsee's levels were shaped by use, mostly by the Mühlendamm weir, which dissected the course of the Spree through the city, channelling trade through the early villages in the region, and more recently by nearby waterworks which draw from the lake. It is at the edge of the city, resting at the borderline of human and natural worlds.

The Leibniz-Institute of Freshwater Ecology has a lab on the shore of Müggelsee. When I'd met with one of their scientists in the autumn – who had told me about Stechlinsee – he'd told me that Müggelsee is so shallow that researchers at the Institute place bets on who can swim in the cold the longest, and when the lake will freeze. In the

nineteenth century, when boating nearby, Fontane reported
a story of a sailor tangled in the weeds and drowning in the
waters here. The placid lake can be deceptive.

The shallowness of Müggelsee is such that, during
spring, summer and autumn, and as wind blows across
the lake's broad surface, the layers of the water often mix
thoroughly, creating a uniform temperature. The lake is
cut through by the flow of the River Spree, further mixing
the water. Its only retreat into stillness is in the solidity of
winter ice, which arrives early and lasts throughout the
season. Lakes like Müggelsee are known as polymictic:
they mix freely, often, as long as there is no ice. They don't
lie still, stratified, like deeper lakes.

By the time I reach Müggelsee, the ice is long gone.
March is streaming with sunshine, the midweek low awash
with gold. I cycle down past Treptow, past Köpenick, until
I reach the forest north-west of the lake. It's both empty
and full: the quiet of a Wednesday shrouded in light, Scots
pine thick and heady in the air. The buds haven't formed
on the oaks yet, but the remnants of the previous year lie
scattered, a thick carpet of mulch.

I cycle round the lake, towards the west, until I reach
a clearing in the reeds. Sand runs up to the pathway,
the fine, golden sand that stretches across Brandenburg.
There's almost no wind today: the lake barely brushes the
shore in small waves. I step out into them, swimming out
in the clarity of the cold. I can see straight to the bottom,
the water's surface barely a border.

Limnology, the study of lakes, takes its name from the
Greek word λίμνη, *limnē*, meaning 'marsh, pool or lake'.

It is a word that stands alone, without an especially telling etymological story.

When I first learned about the field, I was certain that the root *limnē* was related to *limen*, the Latin for threshold or border, but they are false cognates. Saying the word aloud brings recollections to the tongue, the sensation of the word *liminal* arriving as a sister sound, a thought connected by sensation and idea, but not by etymology. *Limen*, however, arrived in English in response to a German word, *Schwelle*, a psychological term referring to the border of the sensible, but also meaning 'threshold' quite materially, like the wood of a door-frame. The German word *Schwelle* links also to water: it can mean an 'accumulation of water' or a 'swell'. The *Deutsches Wörterbuch von Jacob Grimm und Wilhelm Grimm* refers to a swimmer caught in the *Schwelle*, in the swells. This threshold is the space-in-between, the *Zwischenraum*. To me, it is the seam between water and air in a lake. As a swimmer, this is the border of sensation.

That swimming takes place at the boundary between worlds – between lake and land, between nature and culture – stitches the two words together in my mind. Even as I work to learn German, I realise I'm a bad linguist, tangling my words at will. The German word for 'lake' – *See* – recalls the pelagic enormity of the sea. Limnology teaches me not just about lakes, but about borders, about thresholds. In this complicated landscape, it seems appropriate. Many of the lakes here have fluvial waters running through them, making it difficult to determine whether they ought to be considered lakes or wide stretches of river. In Müggelsee, the Spree and the lake intermingle, blurring into one another. The lake, it is said, may take its name from a Proto-Indo-European root: *migh,* for 'fog' or 'cloud'. Vapour afloat.

At the sharp edge of sensation, the cut of the ice, or in the silk of the warming lake, like moments before sleep, the lake is a threshold. Memories swell. Sensation floats at the surface like fog.

The water is a slippery kind of cold: I can sense my toes tightening as I tread it, the clarity of the lake accentuating the shock. There is no pain: it might be the perfect temperature, enough for a rush without the cut of the ice. I can linger at the surface and feel warmth from the sun. I don't rush back to shore. There's a languid possibility in a March swim. I follow the line of the reeds as they curve out along the shore, paddling out until I can't quite see the spot from which I'd entered. It's silent out – just the calls of great tits echoing from the wood, the lapping of the water on the shore-line – and I wonder if I ought to swim back. It's still so shallow I can touch the bottom, just, and so I take my time, floating back to the sand with occasional strokes, sensing the water as it runs over my shoulders.

On the shore again, I dry off as a couple walk by, hand in hand. They stop, watch me with my towel and talk quietly to one another. The sensation of being watched is stronger after having been out in the lake, the solitude of the water and the light a stark contrast with dry land, so I turn and wave. They wander off, spell broken, saying nothing.

I dress and settle for lunch, pour out a steaming cup of coffee, unbox my sandwich. The remnants of the season sit around me, browned oak leaves and crushed fragments of pine cones drying in the sun. Just west of me, the Müggelberge rise, a tree-covered line of hills that create a pocket of shade on the western side of the lake. I make a mental note to come back, to walk the trail up through the hills, to return for a swim.

The bike ride back through the woods and into Köpenick rushes by, and it is midday by the time I reach the bridge over the Dahme River. I've been quick this morning, despite the time I took in swimming, and have some time before I need to get back to the studio to work on my dissertation. I want to enjoy the day, the brightness of late winter, before the season changes. I duck off the road at Alt-Köpenick, turning on to a shaded, cobbled street.

The village sits where the Dahme meets the Spree, its neo-Gothic town hall overlooking the water, made famous in 1906 when a local shoemaker attempted to steal the town's treasury by dressing up as a captain. When Fontane travelled through Brandenburg, he set off from here on a boat journey along the Dahme – known to Fontane as 'the Wendische Spree' – describing his child-like excitement at the trip, the scent of blossom on the air in Köpenick. Today, though, the town is quiet, no flair. It's a Wednesday, and the only people I meet on the streets are older couples strolling slowly along the cobbles. Football flags hang from windows on the side streets. Sunlight cuts the lanes with angles of shadow.

It's beautiful here, but I don't feel fully at ease. Outside the town hall, someone has chalked anti-government and anti-refugee slogans on to the pavement. I see flyers for a counter-protest outside a refugee centre nearby, Berlin's anti-fascist campaigners asking for solidarity against ongoing racism. I skirt past the slogans on the ground, as if my walking away from it might make it disappear. I wonder momentarily when it might rain.

When I was nine, a bank teller in Savannah, Georgia, refused to serve my mother, so my father went inside instead. They served him. I don't know what was said. We waited in the car. I'm halfway between my parents – passing for both and neither – and don't know what I would do. I live in that unsteady balance, a borderland marked on my body. It brings up a kind of uninterrogated discomfort now. I think of how beautiful that town had been too. I think of the new words I'm learning, of the shape my mouth takes when I speak German instead of English, instead of Chinese.

This is the only time I've seen racist graffiti in Berlin – naiveté on my own part – having only ever come across the frequent refrain of *Nazis raus*, 'Nazis Get Out', scrawled across inner city walls. I remember the day Anne and I met, how I hadn't noticed them there on the train platform. And then, as if by instinct, I push the thought back. It's too heavy to hold, and I like this place.

Away and already forgetting, I wheel my bike around to a side street and lock it to a lamp-post by the red-brick church in the centre of town. From here, I follow the line of the sunshine, avoiding the shaded pavement until I pass an inviting café overlooking a wide curve of the road. Sun gleams off the stucco of the building, bright and refracted in the angled, narrow lanes. I step into the coffee-scented air, Edith Piaf playing on a tinny sound system, and take a table by the window. The man behind the counter brings me a bowl of potato soup, which I eat greedily, hungry again despite my earlier lunch, until I feel relaxed, ready to cycle the hour's journey home.

Glancing up, I notice a chalkboard above the counter: *Es fehlt allein der Blick aufs Meer*, 'All that's missing is a view of the sea'. I smile at this, then send the quote to Anne. '*Scheiß-Kitsch!*' she replies. 'Shit kitsch'. I laugh, thinking that's exactly the right term, and exactly why I like it. I pay the bill and make a note to remember this quiet, beautiful lane in Alt-Köpenick, and the sensation of the day.

spring

Overturn: The ice melts, and with the help of the wind the water at the surface mixes with the water at the lake's bottom. The lake reaches a uniform temperature and circulates freely. The lake warms for summer, when it will stratify again.

spring

It's the third weekend in March, the vernal equinox, and Brandenburg hangs with the middling air of early spring, warm but not hot, clouds breaking the brightness of the day. I've reached Königs Wusterhausen, my bike laden with gear: pannier bags filled with food, clothes, my tent and stove. My sleeping bag is strapped to the rack, all of it tied together with a web of straps and buckles. It's surprisingly light despite the load, barely slowing my pace as I push southward along Bahnhofstraße.

I cobbled together this route at the last minute: I'd thought to go east with Coco, cycling towards the Polish border, but she couldn't make it, so I'm heading southward instead. I reach Zeesen and cycle past it, turning down the lane towards Großer Tonteich.

In autumn, the trees here had been thinning, and now they remain stark, bloom not yet arriving. The branches hang tightly, awaiting the moment to unfold themselves, so there's a stillness awaiting warmth, like a breath held. In a week or so, the air will be thick with pollen.

I pass Großer Tonteich, speeding along the southern edge of the asphalt road past the campsite and into the woods, where the trail turns to packed sand. The forest arrives thickly, a stark wall of pine with rough tracks running in every direction. I follow the way to the right and cycle a kilometre past a plantation of spruce, which doesn't grow so well in Brandenburg's sand. It is a small copse, though, all Christmas-tree-sized trunks, a forest in miniature. It ends, and then the forest is just plantation pine: stark and managed industrial forest as far as I can see. I feel suddenly as though I've wandered into a much larger world than the one before, the miniature spruces and sand tracks having turned to towering Scots pine and industrial-scale roads.

The recreational trail disappears and I find myself on a logging road, haphazardly lined with loose cobbles, roughly dumped into the tracks of the lane. The sand to either side is moulded into the wide ridges of tractor tyres, making it impossible to cycle through. I stop for a moment and press my hand into the tyre tracks. Each row of treads is bigger than my hand.

The trees here are bare, lopped so that just their green tops remain. It's a brutal stretch of wood, clearly in the midst of being cut. It's early on a Saturday morning, so no one is at work. I pass an intersection in the logging roads and see a small firepit – a rare sight in the middle of a forest, as fires are strictly regulated in German forests – and a few empty beer bottles and drink cartons wasting into the ground, as if there had been a celebration a few days before I arrived. The trees near the intersection are spray-painted with neon green. It's usually just a stripe, a quick marker denoting trees for cutting or boundaries, but here I see names sprayed on to the trunks. One reads *Tony*, and I wonder where he is now, what he intends to do with the tree he's marked as his.

I'm struggling along the trail, unable to cycle. I'm no better on foot, wheeling my packed bike beside me. The trail is scaled for someone far larger than me. I imagine the logging machine in the animated film *Fern Gully*, which I'd had on VHS when I was six, the diesel-fuelled enormity of the clear-cutting machine. This road is sized for that. I check my map and see that I've another two kilometres before I reach the road. I keep to the edges, where the ground is packed with pine needles.

Fontane travelled through this region by road and water, but for the most part, he travelled in the opposite direction than me, from Spreewald in the south-east of Brandenburg. His journey took him through villages from Wendisch and on towards Blossin, not far from where I eventually reach the main road. Here, the road curves and cuts south-east, on towards the village Groß Eichholz, where it rises steeply and then levels out on to a flat plain.

In Fontane's fourth volume of the *Rambles*, he described the villages of the region as solitary, with ancient pear trees on every lawn, a place of quiet rural living. 'Villages of solitude,' he wrote. My trip through it is much the same, a long and quiet ride, broken only by cobbled village roads where I see no one, but I know much has changed in the intervening years.

I spend the stretches between houses singing medleys of whatever rises from the depths of my mind – Andrew Lloyd Webber musicals and Spice Girls songs woven together – finding a smooth cadence with my pedals.

Then, at the village of Kehrigk, I turn on to a forest track again. The lane takes me past a football field, dusky and overgrown, where three young boys are kicking a dusty ball. One of them kicks it over the fence, and it lands near me on the path. I throw it back over, and though they're speaking to one another in Arabic, the oldest boy turns to me and shouts '*Danke!*' in cheerful German. I smile and watch them play for a while, grabbing a handful of cashews from my bag before cycling off down the track.

A few minutes later, I'm rounding the eastern tip of Neuendorfer See, an enormous, sandy lake in the Unterspreewald region. The road here is freshly laid and black, warm in the afternoon sunlight. It curves with the edge of the lake, dropping me at campground on the lake's shore. Mobile homes stand sentry, awaiting the season. A stark waterfront restaurant overlooks a dock of angling boats, and just one customer sits out front, beer in hand.

I hop off my bike and loosen the kick-stand. Having stopped, my legs are suddenly soft, unstable, forty kilometres into the day. Bending down to the ground, I stretch until I can see the campground behind me, upside down. The man at the restaurant is watching.

I want a quick swim here in this windy stretch of water before I continue onwards towards my campsite. The lake is fairly shallow – not unlike Müggelsee – lined with sticky brown sand, and littered with mussel and clam shells. A few ducks and coots paddle in the shallows by the small beach, but the shore is otherwise quiet. I undress, conscious that I'm being watched from a distance, and then step down into the water. My feet sink into the sandy muck and my muscles tense in the cold, my legs exhausted. I swim out a few feet, not too deep, and dip my head into the water.

On a summer day, I imagine this lake would be beautiful, but far too busy. Now, though, the sun has hidden behind a patch of white clouds – they're dotting the entire sky now – so it feels cold, dim, and I don't stay in long. I dress back on the shore again and then wheel my bike back towards the road, on towards Springsee.

The road towards the campsite is grown-over, a narrow strip running between the pines. Every five hundred metres, a sign informs me that I'm almost there. To my left, fifty metres into the woods, a tall fence runs parallel to the road, signposted with warnings. It's a military training ground. The forest to my right, however, is perfectly planted in parallel rows and seems to run on forever. Ahead of me, the road dips down a steep hill and I find myself at the campground, which sits silently at the shore of Springsee.

The office of the campground is closed, its metal shutters drawn, but I'd called earlier in the day and the owner had kindly suggested I pick any of the tent pitches on the map and set myself up. She would come in on Sunday morning – despite normally being closed – so I could register. At the end of the call, she had complimented my German – she had been very patient with my explaining that I was coming by bike with a tent and that, yes, I knew it would be very cold – and wished me well, so I already felt quite certain I would enjoy my stay.

The gravel lane into the campground slopes towards the lake and then forks into two, with small cabins in one direction and mobile homes in another. Beyond them all, the wooded slopes open up to reveal tent pitches, secluded at the shore of the lake. I pick one near to the path, ten feet from the water, and begin to unpack.

I have my tent up within minutes – I did the complicated work of clipping the fly-sheet and the tent together the last time I had it up – and then look at the time. It's not even half past four, and I've to fill the entire night ahead of me, alone. I've never camped alone. I think of how I would have felt ten years ago, on my own like this. I think of the camping trips I'd planned with Jacob. I momentarily wish for a friend to be with me, but then decide to make the most of the time alone and take a short walk. I lock my bike to a tree near my tent and set off down the lake-side path, collecting twigs for my fire.

Mobile homes and makeshift cabins line the hillside, covered over with deep-green tarps for the winter. For the most part, they remain shut. Just a few people seem to have opened their homes for the spring: there is the distant sound of radio fuzz and a string of fairy lights glowing at the top of the hill. Otherwise, it is quiet. The lake is growing more still and glassy as the minutes slip towards sundown.

Carrying a handful of pine cones and twigs, I walk to the lake's eastern tip, then back again, noticing that three men are now standing on the hillside, watching the path.

I should say 'hello', I think, but I don't quite feel comfortable, so I keep walking, their eyes on the back of me. The path curves around the western tip of the lake, past a rusting condom dispenser – five kinds of condoms and five kinds of lube available at the turn of a metal knob – and up another hill towards a cluster of cabins. Behind me, a couple in a red Volkswagen trundle up the path. I wave at them and continue walking. When I pass by again on my way back, they have unloaded. The man stands on the porch of their cabin trying to light a disposable tray of charcoal.

Back near the centre of the campground, an old man rounds the corner and startles me. I've not expected to see so many people, the place is so silent. He stops me, asking if I've seen his pug, it's lost. He looks frantic, peering up every narrow trail between the cabins. I shake my head and tell him I will look, but as I walk on I hear him greeting his dog with relief, the crisis ended. The place is a series of vignettes.

The sun is beginning to dip towards the horizon, warming the sky to pink. I return to my tent and unpack my stove, pulling out a sachet of dried soup and a bottle of water. Squatting on the ground, I load my stove with a handful of twigs and drop in a crumpled scrap of newspaper, the corner alight. It roars into flame quickly, then peters out, so I feed it some more paper and twigs until it burns steadily. The water boils in minutes, and I pour out half of it for a cup of coffee. The rest I save for lentil soup, which I leave to simmer on the stove. I've packed *Brötchen* too, so tear off the corner of a roll and dip it in my coffee.

The sky over Springsee has grown more saturated, a thick rose hue glowing at the tops of the trees. Contrails from two planes cross overhead, reflecting in the lake, marking treasure in its depths. I leave my soup to cool off a bit and go sit down by the shore, stepping on to the edge of a crooked, ageing dock. I'll swim here in the morning, when it's officially spring. For now, cross-legged, I sip my coffee from a metal cup and watch the sun go down. Watching the lake from here, I think of the dock back at the cottage, where I slip my legs over the far end to see the sunset. It seems strange to me that I was once so afraid of that water, that I hadn't seen the beauty in it.

In past summers, when my best friend Rachel would come to the cottage, we would canoe and sing 'Land Of The Silver Birch'. Rachel knows Canadian camp songs better than anyone, a legacy of months spent at Georgian Bay as a camp counsellor. I imagine that her time spent teaching children to canoe served her well with me, useless with a paddle. The second verse of the 'Land Of The Silver Birch' is about sleeping near the water's edge, the lake 'silent and still', and as I watch the contrails over Springsee fade, I hum to myself quietly. I long for Rachel to be with me, but instead I've a book to keep me company when it is night. Time slows in the silence. Night is slow to come. It's not yet seven.

Back at my tent, the flap tied back, I sit with my legs outside, eating soup from the pot. I over-prepared, packed a tupperware full of marinated tofu as well, so I eat that too. By the end of my meal I'm so exhausted and so full that I zip the tent securely shut and slip into my sleeping bag. The last glint of light still hangs over the pines across the way, and the tent still lets in the faint glow of the sky.

I pull out my spare bike light – using it as a book torch – and dip back into my novel. I'm nearing the end of *The Tiger's Wife* – thick in its stories of the lone tiger in the woodland, post-war village fields trapped with land-mines – when the sound starts. A low patter at first, like oil spluttering in a pan, but then louder, like fireworks breaking up into the sky. I lie still and listen. There's only darkness outside, but then the sound comes again, echoing this time, a sound like gunfire ripping into the forest across from me. It takes me a moment to recognise that it *is* gunfire – or blanks, at least – coming from the military training ground nearby. It's the site used by the Bundeswehr for combat training. I'd seen signs posted nearby, but I hadn't realised it was this close.

Since the taxi accident, I've been terrified by loud sounds – fireworks, the pop of a balloon, the blaring horn of a passing car – and have struggled to regain my calm in those startled moments, as terror returned with every unexpected sound. But now, the gunfire pattering in the distance, I'm okay. I lie for some minutes, listening to their ripple and crack over the silent lake, and then go back to reading. I've found some fragment of strength in the solitude.

I fall asleep at some point, but am awoken by a dog calling from the lake. I think of the lost pug and then remember he's been found. The sound comes again, but it isn't a dog – it is coming from the water, a coot perhaps, barking in the night. Something rustles outside my tent, and I begin to worry about my bike being stolen.

I sit shivering – it's just three degrees overnight – until I decide to get up, peer outside my tent and tie the flysheet to my bike bell. I slip out into the darkness and find it more silent than before, even the coots have gone. I laugh at myself momentarily, but then tie the thin cord to the bell anyway, knowing that I'll sleep better if I'm tied to my bike and to a sound I'll recognise.

I grow restless in the night, cold creeping through my sleeping bag – I'm at its lower temperature limit – and into the air. In some moments I'm awake, pressing the button on my light so I can see my breath cloud in the cold air, and then I'm in a dream-like haze, my mind racing with thoughts of the tent zipper sliding upwards, what I might do. I manage some rest until five, when the sky should turn from black to slate blue, and then push my head out of the tent to find that the world is grey, prickled with cold rain.

I'm worn out from the night, gazing at the lake, now rippling and dark. It had been so beautiful the night before, and I immediately regret not swimming then. But it is technically spring, and I want to celebrate it with a swim. Springsee – *spring* in German can mean a fluvial 'spring' or, simply, 'to jump' – seemed an apt choice.

I slip into the lake naked – no one else is around – and swim out into the centre. It seems warmer here, the lake less rippled by rain, so I linger a while, letting the cold wake my limbs. I feel my skin tighten, my mind sharpen – it feels the same as caffeine but clearer, more visceral – and then swim back to shore, rushing back to the relative warmth of my tent. I dress inside, trailing bits of leaf and dirt in after me, and then light my stove to make breakfast.

Once my porridge is cooked, I shelter halfway inside

my tent, warming my hand over the fire while I spoon hot porridge into my mouth with the other. I've downed a cup of coffee and am racing through the porridge, burning my tongue. The wet spring morning is so cold, but I am warm.

ember

Late the next Friday evening, the sky occluded with grey, I take the train to Frankfurt an der Oder. It rains the whole way, the same cold, miserly drizzle that has lingered since spring arrived. The train is a slow-moving local, stopping frequently as it winds its way through the countryside south-east of the city. It traces the same routes I cycled last week on my way to Springsee, before cutting north-east again towards the Polish border.

I try to gaze out the window, but there's only blackness outside and the beading of rain on the glass. I watch the carriage instead, the teenagers riding from one stop to another, a young woman reading a paperback. It's a one-carriage train, stark but intimate. I shouldn't be taking the trip. My dissertation is due at the end of the month, and I should be spending every minute at work. For a while, I balance my laptop on my knees and work, but the sound of my keyboard clacking echoes through the carriage. I grow self-conscious and return to watching the darkness outside the window. The other passengers watch me like I watch them, furtively, out of the corners of their eyes.

When I reach Frankfurt an der Oder – a town just on the Polish border at the banks of the Oder River, which lends its name to help distinguish the town from Frankfurt am Main – the rain has lifted. It is lamp-lit and silent in the town. I wheel my bike to a nearby hotel and check into a stark, simple room with starched sheets. There's a television with a handful of German channels, all playing historical documentaries late at night. One of them is about a castle, I think, so I let it play for a while. I don't have a TV at home, so I spend time on every channel, delighting at the glow in the darkened room before falling into sleep. Tonight is a brief stop-over, a small luxury I'm affording myself on my way to Helenesee. I'd wanted a night away from the city, a break in the monotony of proof-reading and editing. The anonymity of the budget hotel room feels grounding, oddly restorative.

The morning is bright, the grey has gone at last. I wake up early, eat *Brötchen* and boiled eggs for breakfast, and set out, first winding my bike through the small centre of town, towards the river. I pass a handful of gothic-style brick buildings and then find myself on a small side road leading to Ziegenwerder, a small island in the Oder, overlooking Poland. It is said that the island once served as pasture for goats – *Ziegen* means 'goats' – brought here by their herder, Gottlieb. The island's soft grasses fed the goats of the city for some time, until, local legend says, the herder fell in love with a young beauty across the water and sought to make his way across. The effort ended badly.

The river is wide. I gaze across it, towards the Polish town of Slubice, once a part of Frankfurt an der Oder, where flat stretches of grass south of the town glint in the sunlight. The Oder is wide and glassy, flowing steadily. I walk the length of the island. There used to be a bathing club here too, swimming off the banks of the island.

I wheel my bike up a cobbled lane and back to the main road, cycling down towards Helenesee. It takes me forty minutes, keeping to the bike lane on a busy road, until I reach the quiet trail and turn off, following the track between dormant fields. The thick stench of garbage permeates the air along the lane, and I soon pass a dump, piles of waste stacked and rotting. I push past it, launching myself into the forest ahead and into the pine air.

The forest opens on to a paved road, the fence of a campsite running parallel into the distance. I cycle down around the fence, finding the gates closed, and then follow the road westward, around the curve of Helenesee. I can't see the lake – the road is set far back – but I know it's there. There's a spot of clear sky in the centre of the tree-line, the open space of the water.

Around the western side of the lake, a gap between the fences opens and I find my way into a row of neatly managed pines. A short way in, the trees break and I see the vast, glittering surface of Helenesee open beneath me, sunken beneath the hillside. It takes up the entirety of the horizon, stretching far into the distance and from side to side. It seems strange, now, that the trees had hidden it so well. The lake is enormous.

I'm surprised momentarily by two walkers on the path. Two older men clad in hiking gear are admiring the scope

of the view as well, and they greet me politely before following a trail southward around the lake. I stay where I am
near the trees. It's too steep to take my bike, so I leave it at
the top of the hill and slip down the steep banks towards
the lake-shore.

The banks here are so steep in part because they aren't
natural. Helenesee, like many of the clear-watered lakes
in Brandenburg left by quarries and mines, was created
in the middle of the twentieth century. The steep banks
originally marked the edges of Grube Helene, one of the
many lignite mines in the region.

Lignite deposits, or brown coal, in eastern Germany,
especially Brandenburg's south-east, are among the most
plentiful in the world. Lignite is found where peat bogs
developed fifteen to twenty million years ago and came
under pressure from glaciers. So like many of Brandenburg's
lakes, the story of lignite is traced back to ice.

The deposits were discovered in the eighteenth century, and by the middle of the nineteenth century, as
Germany rapidly industrialised, lignite became a key
source of energy. Opencast mines were established across
the south-east of Brandenburg, and by the end of the
1940s, coal deposits were one of East Germany's richest
natural resources. In the 1970s, when oil prices rose, it
became more crucial than ever to the economy of the East.
Coal was burned in domestic ovens across the country.
Combined with the oily blue fumes emitted by the Trabis
(the popular East German cars), the air quality of the East
declined drastically. Acid rain damaged forests across the
east of Europe, depleting the already poor tree stocks of
Brandenburg, but still, in discussion with the Swedish

prime minister, East German leader Erich Honecker famously declared that there was no acid rain in the GDR. Lignite was essential.

As the region around Frankfurt Oder industrialised in the late nineteenth and early twentieth centuries, lignite was required to fuel the new and busy factories for jam and glass production. After a series of earlier mines were created, Grube Helene was opened in 1943, adjacent to the earlier opencast mine Grube Katja. It was mined until 1958, at which point the open pit was filled with ground-water and began the slow process of becoming Helenesee, the lake as it is today. By 1970, it was complete.

I've glanced over old photos of men stood underground, carts of coal next to them. My grandfather was a coal miner in Wales and my great uncle a coal deliveryman. My father told me stories of Uncle Ronnie turning up to the house covered in coal dust, brown-black creased into his skin. The pictures of miners at Grube Helene remind me of them. The residue of coal emanates from the photographs, reminds me of family, but they both seem distant when I'm stood on the shores of Helensee, bright as it is. There is nothing of coal remaining.

The shore of the lake is sparse and sandy, lined occasionally with scrim – grasses and reeds that are beginning to take root along the shore – but the impression is stark, bright, beautiful. I step out into the water, and it has the same kind of sharp clarity that I'd found at Müggelsee. The men out for a hike have disappeared into the forest, and I'm completely alone at the base of this hill, in the face of this enormous swathe of reflective blue. Sun drifts overhead and then disappears behind a thin gauze of cloud.

I swim out, the cold rising over my shoulders with a crisp shock. It's freezing despite the sun, a product of the water's intense clarity. The lake is poor in plankton, has little algae and doesn't hold heat all that well. It has very few plants – Elodea and water milfoil have taken root in nearby Katja See, but not here. Instead, I watch the empty sand pass at a distance beneath me.

When scientists study the clarity of a body of water, one of the tools they use is a Secchi disc. The circular disc – invented by the Italian scientist Angelo Secchi in 1865 – is plunged into a shaded patch of water until it is no longer visible. The depth at which it disappears is used to calculate the water's turbidity, how far light reaches in a lake and how well plants can survive. The greater the Secchi depth, the clearer the water. Temperature in a lake is shaped by a multitude of factors – shape, wind, sun, sediment – but one of those is turbidity. The less clear a lake, the more its many particles absorb heat and impact the lake's life cycle. The turbid lakes freeze more readily come winter. In clear lakes, over time the temperature will warm up, the sunlight reaching deeper into its depths, leaving it ice-free for longer come winter. Bizarrely enough, at the end of cold season, a deep, clear lake can stay frozen for longer than a shallower, cloudier one, as its temperature changes more slowly.

I think about this as I swim out into the Helenesee. The water has an immaculate clarity to it, not sterile but immensely clean. Fifty-five metres at its deepest point, I feel as if I could always see straight to the bottom.

I linger a while, feeling small in the pit of the lake, the scooped-out, wide feeling of the horizon here, and then trace my way back to shore. I dress and scramble up the steep hillside where my bike awaits, and then I set out, beginning the eighty-kilometre journey back to town. It will take the rest of the day.

The road away from Helenesee is empty. I cycle as fast as I can, picking up speed on the slick asphalt, watching the light tick between trees as I pass them. I swerve, narrowly missing a toad that sits in the middle of the road, and then I begin to notice them. For a kilometre or so, toads have wandered on to the warmth of the country road and been flattened by cars. Some have been spared and linger by the road's edges, but most are splattered, belly up and drying in the spring warmth.

Common toads follow the same yearly route to their ancestral breeding sites, whether or not the route takes them over the road. On this stretch, for the past few years conservationists have been installing plastic fences, low to the ground, punctuated by sunken buckets into which the toads will drop. A few times a day, workers come out and carry the buckets of toads safely across the road to their breeding grounds, an ingenious but not entirely convenient effort to spare the toads. Not all of them make it. I stop and examine a few who have made it to the roadside alive, getting on my knees to look at them from eye-level, and then cycle on, trying in vain to avoid the dead ones as they dot the ground.

The route back to Berlin takes me through Müllrose, a town that sits along the Oder-Spree canals, and then on along the bike route that follows Spree, through a forest of birch and sparse pine. I cross a ramshackle wooden bridge over the river, and then find myself on the cobbled streets of Fürstenwalde, a town at a ford of the Spree. I stop at a supermarket on the edge of town and buy cheese and pretzels, which I eat greedily outside in the car park. Passing shoppers stare as they wander in for their weekend shop. I don't care, though. I pack an extra packet of cheese into my back-pack and retie my hair. I've another few hours ahead of me on the bike, so I refill my water bottle and set out again.

The stretch towards Erkner, on the edge of Berlin, is a long one, and I occupy it by singing. I pick a record and sing it track by track until I'm through, and then pick another and sing that one. I'm breathless by the end of it, but it keeps my mind from overthinking, from spinning away in time with my bicycle. The past weeks have shifted something, the sting of anger gone and the hurt of the past lessened. The heat of my feelings has abated, cooled to a soft glow, a steady emanation, no flares, no fire. Cycling home to Berlin, there's a calm in the distance, in the blankness of my mind as I cycle and sing, and I'm grateful for it at last.

bridge

It's late in the morning when we meet at Nordbahnhof. We were out the night before, a Friday night dinner at one of the cosiest but loudest restaurants in Mitte. Anne and her friends had gathered at the restaurant long before me. This past month I've been so thick in work preparing to submit my dissertation, due in three weeks, I've been late for everything. I arrived at the restaurant flustered, my vision blurred from work and my mind still writing in English, and was launched immediately into a dinner-time conversation in German. I spent most of the meal catching up, trying and failing to follow, asking *'Wie bitte?'*, and swallowing my words. Frustrated, I turned my focus instead to the plate of *Käsespätzle* in front of me.

A feeling of homesickness has been hanging over me – the same undefinable, amorphous feeling that I'd carried around in summer – and dinner in another language magnified it. Berlin has become home in so many ways, but I've been missing my old friends, missing London and

Toronto. In substitute I've been living online, communicating in one-hundred-and-forty-letter fragments, talking through FaceTime windows. On Skype, a close friend said to me that this is not how humans are supposed to live, but to me the screen has become a familiar place, a hollow landscape in itself, flaring bright as the lakes. In that world, my German is auto-corrected.

Somewhat recovered from the shock of dinner, I sit on the S-Bahn platform at Nordbahnhof drinking coffee from my thermos. Anne is showing me her new vintage bicycle – a sleek pink and black relic with down-tube gear levers – which she has just bought to replace the rusting old one she's been riding since she was a teenager. It's bittersweet. The new one is a joy to ride, she tells me, but I understand her longing for familiarity. The old bicycle is unfixable; I suggest she keep it as a souvenir anyway, though I wonder where she'll store it.

We board the train and take it to the end of the line. When we emerge at Wannsee, the station is crowded with tourists and families, but we wind our way through and cycle down towards the Glienicke Bridge. Its seafoam-hued steel hangs gracefully across the Havel: modest, low, sloping curves that obfuscate their own importance. We have to dismount and walk; the bridge is covered with tourists, darting across the road to snap pictures of themselves at the bridge's centre. Anne rolls her eyes.

'Tom Hanks fans,' she mumbles, and I suppress a laugh. It's more crowded than the station had been. A family of tourists have posed on one side of the bridge, one of their own having crossed over to snap the photo from a distance. We wander across, weaving between them, pausing now and then to avoid walking into the gaze of other people's cameras.

Glienicke Bridge marks the present border between Berlin and Brandenburg. Until recently, it marked the border between east and west, was the bridge between worlds, the bridge constantly at the centre of negotiations. It is the famous bridge for trading spies between the Americans and the Soviets. It's a tiny arc of iron, in reality.

On the other end, we follow the road along the water, sloping down towards Jungfernsee, and into Neuer Garten. Lenné, who designed the gardens at Petzow, where we'd been a few weeks back, redesigned the gardens here in 1816. As we cycle through, Anne remarks that the world is coming back to life in the spring air: everything is trimmed in the faintest green. Daffodils rise from the cropped lawns at the path's edge. It's April – they're late. I'm thinking of St David's Day, of my Welsh grandparents. I'd always brought them daffodils at the beginning of March.

We cycle on along the water, passing a small quay where a cluster of river freighters are tied together. The saline smell of the boats and the water wafts up between them. Rust peels from their sides. Anne stops, transfixed. Lobbing her bike on the lawn, she asks me to stop for a moment. She climbs aboard the nearest ship.

'We're going to get in trouble!' I whisper, though there's no one around. She turns and gives me the same look she gave the tourists, all eyes and pursed lips. She calls me a goody goody. Climbing fences is no matter to me, but the freighters make me nervous. I worry about slipping between their cracks, into the metal-edged darkness below. A part of me worries about being an interloper, being caught offside. Glancing around for onlookers, I follow her aboard, ducking under a thick railing rope.

She walks to the edge of the first boat and takes a broad step on to the next, working her way towards the water's edge. I hang back, watching, standing by the ship's wheel. Anne takes photographs, crouching down low on the iron floor, while I urge her to hurry up. A mechanical hum is drifting around the corner of the trees. Another small freighter approaches, looking to tie up next to us.

'Come on!' I call, and we slip back on to dry land and on to our bikes. We pedal out of sight just as the other boat slips alongside the freighters. We carry on quietly, searching for the right place to swim. A few hundred yards along, we find a bench and a clearing, a fallen willow leaning out over the lake, half in leaf. We stop here, locking our bikes to themselves and clambering down the small ledge overlooking the water. Jungfernsee is clear, just sand and mussels dotting the lake's bottom. A short way out, fallen logs break the surface.

I throw my back-pack to the ground and wander towards the willow. It's damp, its thin layers of moss still holding on to prior rain, so I slip off my shoes and step sock-footed on to the bark. Crouching low, I work my way out over the water, into the thickening branches of the tree. Once I'm halfway out, I pause to take a photograph, and then turn to see that Anne is photographing me from the shore. She crouches at the edge of the water, her camera held aloft, eyes focused. I stay still a moment and then turn to climb down, but find it steeper than I'd imagined and have to shimmy down, gripping the width of the tree for support. When I reach the ground, my socks are soaked through from the moss.

'I love trees like this,' I say as I reach the ground. 'They always remind me of *Bridge to Terabithia*.'

'What's that?' Anne asks me, and I'm momentarily surprised, but then remember that we grew up half a world apart, in completely different languages. I begin to explain the plot of the book, a waypoint in North American childhood, and then stop short. I say only that fallen trees, to me, always mean magic, friendship and escape. I speak about childhood and nostalgia. But I don't speak about tragedy. I think of the timelessness of the tree over the water, the golden light cast by memory. When I finish, Anne tells me that Jungfernsee means 'Virgin's Lake', and we laugh.

We pile our clothes by the waterside and step out, the cool of early spring rising to our chests. Small clusters of slick green hornwort dot the shallows. Left alone, they'll grow up and choke the lake. I swim around them, dodging the sunken logs, and move towards the centre of the lake. Another small freighter is making its way down the corridor of Jungfernsee. It's a narrow arm of the Havel and sits on a federal waterway, making it popular with tourist boats and freighters alike. I swim a while longer in the deep. A tourist boat passes, and I wave from the water.

Afterwards, dressed again, Anne and I regain warmth on the shore, eating our lunch and drinking from our thermos flasks. It's grey, a slight drizzle drifting in over the lake, but we're sheltered beneath trees. The bench at the shore is a concrete monolith, slowly growing over with lichen. I wrap myself cross-legged atop it and we chat, lingering for what feels like an hour.

At dinner the night before, the discussion had turned to old-fashioned names, the names that none of us could take seriously on a date. Friends had offered suggestions: Fritz or Gudrun. But I struggled to hear the difference between old-fashioned German names and, say, Hannes or Eva. We turn back to the topic now, sitting by the lake, and I try to list names I think would be old-fashioned in English. All of them, I explain, are being used again. Anne and I run back and forth offering suggestions, laughing about how Fritz would sound during sex, which names sound trashy in America or Britain, and which sound posh. I complain about my name, but if I hadn't been Jessica I would have been Michelle, and I don't like that any better. I teach Anne to pronounce my Chinese name: the upwards rise of the *Jie*, the downwards fall of the *Ke*. It isn't official, doesn't appear on any documents, but it is mine, given to me by my mother, like so much in my life. I love it.

Names are haphazard, I realise. Every time I offer a name for discussion, Anne responds with surprise. She gives a German one and we both laugh.

We turn to talk of friends, of friends we've gained and friends we've lost, and I realise how new our friendship is. I realise how much it has come to mean to me, someone swimming through the cold alongside me, asking for nothing but my company. Offering hers. A steady presence.

I watch the coots fish in the shallows, point out a heron wading amidst the logs, and then we pack up, ready to cycle back.

It begins to rain again as we retrace our route through Neuer Garten. We take shelter briefly at the Meierei and then cycle on, out of the gardens, back towards the Glienicke Bridge. The whole day, we've been pointing to houses we like and suggesting we live in them. The area is awash with villas, enormous stone houses overlooking the water, and modernist cubes positioned for the view. We've been taking our pick. Just imagine swimming here every morning, Anne says. Outside Neuer Garten we spot another one – a sandstone villa overlooking the water – and it is for sale. I pull out my phone and check the agent's website. Five million euros. It's possible our freelancer budgets won't stretch to that, I remark, and we cycle on, still laughing.

We follow the Mauerweg back, ducking northwards after crossing the Glienicke Bridge. The trail takes us downwards, towards lake-level, and runs along the Havel. We run into the nearby forest and then back out again, along a beach where the sky is split with a crack between storm clouds and sun. It is one of the middling, unsure days of early spring; the sky can't decide what it wants to do. The view over Jungfernsee, just on the horizon, is swathed in black. Towards Wannsee is blue and sun.

We cycle onwards, down a track that has sprung to life in the rain, the smell of wild garlic hanging thickly in the air. I've been this way before, once, with Jacob, along the Havel past the Pfaueninsel – the eighteenth-century landscape garden on an island, famous for its peacocks, and for its design by Lenné – and towards Wannsee. It had been one of those days, the kind I remember in vivid detail, every moment worth an age. But now, with Anne, I feel freer. I could forget this day, though I know I won't, and it wouldn't make it any less valuable. The burden of memory is lighter. I breathe in the allium scent of the ground and suggest, impulsively, that we stop and swim again. The sun is out. Wannsee is blue as ever.

I hadn't intended to swim in Wannsee in part because of its ubiquity. I'd wanted to pursue lakes at a distance, lakes lesser known and lakes I'd not been to before. But the day, which had been so grey at Jungfernsee, is becoming so bright.

Wannsee is, perhaps, Berlin's most famous lake. Anne begins to sing '*Pack Die Badehose Ein*'. Connie Froboess's 1951 song about Wannsee perhaps embodies its importance to West Berliners. The song will be stuck in my head for a week. A bight of the Havel, its northern banks are taken up with the yellow-bricked 1920s *Strandbad*. It sits authoritatively on the opposite side from us, the sanctioned swimming place, sprawling and serious. We stand instead at the edge of a forest clearing, where a dock extends into the water. Pfaueninsel sits to the west. On the northern horizon, I can just make out the white-domed top of Teufelsberg, no longer listening to the city below. The forest around us is oak and pine.

I strip out of my clothes and walk naked on to the dock. It's warm in the sunlight, and the water here is so clear I can see straight to the bottom. A *No Diving* sign marks the end of the dock, but the lake is clear and there is no one around. I spring, knees flexing, and hit the water smoothly, a pointed, shallow dive into the blue cold. When I surface, two men passing on a nearby boat are applauding. I hadn't seen them watching.

Anne follows me out into the water, swimming out into the distance where the water runs so deep it feels bottomless. It's the cleanest sensation of wetness, sharper than Jungfernsee, though their waters flow together from the Havel. Wannsee feels different, more like the fine and bevelled edge of a glass held to the light. On my back, my breasts and toes floating just above the lake's surface, I feel the border between the sun and the water, a golden warmth and evaporating blue cold running together. I bask there a while, hands gliding at my sides and then resting on my tummy, otter-like, still. I turn to Anne and see that she's been watching me swim.

'The adoration of the sun,' she says smiling.

'Exactly.'

The winter is a memory already, the spring now fully formed, verdant and vital. Out in Wannsee, we linger longer than ever before, the cold turning to comfort. We breathe in the sunlight and prepare for summer. The blue-soaked warmth of it, the softened blanket of the water on our bodies.

slope

Anne is crouched reading the names on the doorbells when I leave my house, a five-storey stucco block in Prenzlauer Berg. My name is written all in capitals, three short black letters next to a silver button. Anne is running her finger over the names above and below: Kandinsky, Richter, Picasso.

'Artists' house,' she says.

'They're all rentals,' I tell her. I've moved again, this time into my own one-room apartment in the inner courtyard of a quiet building. It has rough wooden floors and a small terrace off the kitchen. The neighbours are all holiday-makers, changing by the week. My name is on the door. I imagine this means I'll stay.

It's clouding over a bit as we cycle away. I've not swum in ten days – focusing thoroughly on work in the final push for my dissertation, which I've completed at last. It feels like the last moment of an exhalation, small and sputtering, and anti-climactic. Anne and I have been saving this journey for a good day, as if to celebrate, so I hope it clears.

We bike to Lichtenberg, Anne racing ahead on her bicycle, which she has nicknamed 'Bonnie Tyler'. Last week, on our way back from dinner, I'd cycled behind her singing 'Total Eclipse Of The Heart', racing to keep up. Today is no different. We dart through the traffic along Danziger Straße as we work our ways towards Frankfurter Tor. We cut southwards, dodging pedestrians lingering in the bike lane. We reach the train station early, giving us time to wait on the platform ahead of our train east.

The carriage is full, bikes lined into the aisles as day trippers make their way towards the city's edge. The S-Bahn along this route is closed today, so the regional trains are packed. Everyone jostles for space, bikes clinking against one another as they're rammed up close alongside the carriage sides. We find a small corner to stand with our bikes and wait for the crowds to clear. It doesn't take long. Near Strausberg, the train empties and we have the carriage to ourselves for the journey towards Müncheberg, halfway to the Polish border.

We're headed to Schermützelsee, a crook-shaped lake in the Märkische Schweiz, one of the lakes Fontane most loved. When I'd read the *Rambles*, I had lingered over his descriptions of the lakes there: the blue crescent of the Schermützelsee, the slope of the tree-lined hills plummeting down towards the water. That had been enough to convince me.

Anne, like me, has done her research. The lake is in Buckow – we'll bike to the town from Müncheberg station, about ten kilometres – and as we ride the train Anne lingers over the etymology of the town's name.

'Buckow,' she says. 'The -ow. I've been telling you about these endings, the Slavic ones.' I nod. Indeed, as we've unravelled the etymology of lake and town names over the recent months, the -ow suffix has come up before. The suffix, Anne explains, is just an indication for 'settlement'. Buckow, from the German 'Buche' translates to 'beech settlement': the village with many beeches. Anne is sliding through pages on her iPad as the train rolls towards Müncheberg.

'The -ow, though, it's like the German -aue.' She is immersed, piecing together word parts the way I piece together the landscape from scraps of moss, bits of flower. She laughs at me when I crouch to the ground to look at plants, but I think that this moment with the iPad is her version of it. She has a doctorate in literature and a penchant for the mundanities of German etymology. Last week over dinner she had taught me the word for 'saucer', *Untertasse*, 'under-cup', glowing at its simplicity, its functionality, lifting the tea-cup in the crook of her finger as if to emphasise her point. She keeps reading.

'The -aue, it's often used for things that are near water. Not the water and not the field, but a meadow or pasture close to water.'

'A marsh?' I offer.

'No.'

Later, she'll send me the transcript of a Deutschlandradio Kultur show with an expert on Brandenburg place names. Etymologically, the Slavic and German suffixes -ow and -aue are completely different. The -aue, I'll read, was for centuries imposed on places with Slavic names, one of the many historical means of Germanising the land-scape. German rule spread to Brandenburg in the twelfth century, and the complexity of place names still reflects this. -aue, linked to the Latin *aqua*, indicates water, a wet meadow. Now, the region is awash with these muddled place names. I think of the more recent wave of name changes, the story of Gütergotz. I think of my own name, written in English, written in Chinese.

We pull into Müncheberg and wheel our bikes on to the cobbled road by the station. The lane leads north, through a hedge-lined patchwork of fields, rising up and sloping downwards in ways unlike the rest of Brandenburg. It is not without reason that the region is called the Märkische Schweiz: it is the 'Switzerland' of Brandenburg. The hills are Brandenburg's Alpine analogue.

Fontane's second volume of the *Rambles* took him to Buckow. His is a world of rising hills, larch, fir and blackberry lining the landscape. Fontane's Buckow is a 'rural beauty' bathing in the lake barefooted, hair braided beneath a willow tree. The red-tiled roofs of the village sit nestled into the hillside next to the silent stillness of Schermützelsee. It is a landscape of impenetrable quiet, of beauty and of memory. For Fontane, stories unfold in the landscape, time is compressed. Memory is layered like leaves, like pages.

Literary critics have argued that Fontane's Brandenburg is a unified landscape, its flat fields and waterways easily traversed, with no true obstacles. In the face of rapid industrial change and urban growth, his landscape is a place of intimacy, the landscape of the walker. The rivers and the lakes are markers of Brandenburg's unity, stitches and seams that run across the land. Now, Anne and I are trundling across this landscape, across a stitched-together patchwork of lane, hedgerow and hillside. It is rolling and quaint, a place scaled for walkers, for bicycles. I think, for a moment, I am in England, but then we pass a man on the roadside, clad in a canvas apron, working in his garden. He looks up and greets us.

'*Guten Morgen!*' I am in Brandenburg. A thin stand of Scots pine opens up ahead of me, a constant reminder of this place, the species that covers three-quarters of the state's forest. The hills plummet downwards – I'd mapped this route earlier, traced the elevation on Google Maps, remembered the drop – and we wind our way, curving with the lane, into the valley towards Buckow. The lane looses us on to a cobbled road in the village, with just the small Eisenbahn-Museum and the single-carriage, still dormant Kleinbahn railway waiting for summer. The barn doors to the museum are open on their slides, the workers inside painting and preparing for the coming season. It smells of turpentine. The burgundy and beige Kleinbahn lies static, appearing disused. In a week's time, it will run the route between Buckow and Müncheberg, a connection between this otherworldly pocket of the Märkische Schweiz and the train lines to Berlin. It's run this route since 1897, though today it mostly carries tourists.

The cobbled road leads us further downhill, a steep and sloping curve. I hadn't thought we could go lower. At the bottom sits the slate-blue plate of Schermützelsee, greying beneath the lightly clouded sky. In summer, this lake turns turquoise in the light, and as today's clouds break and sun hits the surface, there are glints of colour. It's still early.

We follow the road around the northern side of the lake, down on to a dirt track scattered with holiday homes, their wooden docks extending out into the lake. Anne is enraptured. She points to the houses she would like, the gardens slipping down towards the water. Every piece of land here feels enclosed, cosy, unlike the stark and unravelled immensity of the rest of Brandenburg.

We dodge off the trail and into the forest, the sloping sides of which Fontane lingered over, the branches of trees dipping down towards the water, all of which to him most embodied the rural quaintness of the Märkische Schweiz. The forest here is scattered with alder trees, their wide, paw-shaped leaves just unfolding. The ground is speckled with pink sprays of common toothwort, its parasitic inflorescences reaching just above the soil and rotting leaves. Ivy has spread over the forest in patches, and the spaces between trees reveal occasional signs of use: a bottle cap, a receipt. The forest is quiet but not unused.

We find a clearing in the trees where the forest opens into the sparse lake floor. From the water's edge, the red-tiled houses of Buckow are just visible, dotted amidst the trees. I imagine it as Fontane saw it. Anne points to the houses along the slopes.

'Which is Brecht-Weigel Haus, do you think?' Bertolt Brecht and the actress Helene Weigel had a summer house here. I scan over the white-walled houses and tile roofs, pointing to one with a steep roof and wide windows overlooking the lake.

'That one,' I guess. I'm wrong, in any case, but for now we are satisfied. We pile our clothes by an alder tree and step out into the lake, already warming in the spring air.

I swim out a way, watching the sky for sun, but the clouds don't break. The sun is dulled behind a blanket of cirrostratus, turning the lake a dull kind of blue. The farther I swim, though, the richer the colour becomes. Fifty feet out, the depth turns the lake to a deep emerald – the kind of colour I know from Liepnitzsee in the sun – and I'm transported to summer. Anne swims out too, taking broad, graceful strokes at the lake's surface. She swims farther out than me, towards the clouded sun, while I return to shore. I watch her while I towel off and get dressed. She is in her own world, transported by the lake to somewhere distant. I call out to her.

'Don't swim too far!' She turns towards me and makes a wide circle in the water. Her movement is steady.

When she returns to shore, I wander along the trail for a few minutes, finding an enormous birch with a rope swing attached. The cries of past summers hang over the place. Soon, it won't be so silent.

Anne is sitting on a bare log drinking tea and eating Halloren-Kugeln, from the oldest chocolate factory in Germany, opened in 1804. She hands me the packet and I draw the chocolate to my mouth, the thick cream sweetness of it slipping over my tongue. Halloren chocolates, she explains, were incredibly popular in the GDR, one of the few brands that withstood reunification. Anne is always turning up with chocolates I've never heard of, sweets I've never seen before. An interpreter, a guide. The sweets all have a story, a memory attached. I suppose I could do the same, given a Dairy Milk or box of maple creams. The past is at the tips of our tongues.

We cycle back, retracing our route, and then turn off

at the signs pointing towards Brecht-Weigel Haus. The house is at the base of a deep hillside, its red-tiled roof reaching down towards the ground. The façade is painted with white and green looping curls, and wooden shutters line the windows. The gate is locked. The museum won't open for another hour. I ask Anne if she'd like to wait, but she shakes her head, takes a photograph through the gate.

'We'll come back!' she sings, and then we return to our bikes, following the track towards Buckowsee. It is a small, glassy mirror at the base of the town, the church and the roofs doubled in a watery plate. Boardwalks lead along the Sophienfließe stream stemming from the small lake, and beyond the small lawn leading to the water stands a series of placards and rocks in a stylised curve. This is the Eiszeitgarten, a small display of glacial erratics set up to illustrate the movement of glaciers across the landscape of northern Europe. The rocks here are marked with labels, their ages identified, their variety named: granite, sandstone, chalk, porphyritic rock. Fontane too had been preoccupied with geology at Buckow, the situation of the lake and its valley in a glacial kettle. The rippling, crenulated shore of the Schermützelsee points to its origin as a dead-ice kettle. Kettle lakes formed when glaciers left ice behind in their retreat, the way plaster fills a mould, leaving their form behind as the land masses surrounding them settled. The rolling hills of the Märkische Schweiz were formed through a myriad of such retreats in the Weichselian glaciation, the last time ice covered northern Europe, between one hundred thousand and ten thousand years ago. I pick my way through the rocks in the garden, pressing my hand on each of them; enormous stones brought here to illustrate glacial advance and retreat in miniature. They come from as far away as the middle of Sweden, carved away by ice and blasted by sand. The stories of their travels are written on their surfaces. Erratics came from far away, but they helped shape this place.

We cycle onwards, along the Sophienfließe and back through town, finding our way towards Großer Däbersee, Anne's suggestion. The lake, also a glacial remnant, sits south of Buckow, along the quiet residential streets of Waldsieversdorf. It's a secluded lake, lined on three sides by forest and reeds. A simple *Strandbad* with a dock sits on its northern shore, and it is here that we lock our bikes. The nearest entry to the lake is through the beach, but it is ticketed in summer. We enquire at the café by the beach and the woman is so surprised we're swimming – the season won't officially begin for another week – that she encourages us in, waives the ticket fee. Satisfied, we make our way down to the dock and strip off, readying ourselves for the depth of the water. My swimsuit is wet from Schermützelsee, so I strip down to my underwear and walk to the edge of the dock, arms suspended for a dive. On the terrace by the café, two men sit drinking coffee, overlooking us by the lake. Inside, behind the glassy windows, a family sits eating their lunch.

With a quick flick, I enter the water, no longer a cold shock. I surface and swim out towards the sun. It looks like home, like the cottage, lined by pines on all sides. I've no fear of the dock, the depth, the darkness. It slips over me as I slip down into it.

Anne is more tentative. She climbs down the rusting

ladder and into the opaque sheet of the lake. I remember this fear, these tentative steps into oblivion, but they seem so far away for me as I tread water in Großer Däbersee. The unknowable blackness of it lies beneath me. I love this lake, its hemmed-in feeling of familiarity, its crooked shore. The hook in my heart.

Dressed again, we sit on the benches by the café drinking coffee. I crack the shell of a boiled egg and eat it as I watch the shore. The family sitting by the window gets up to leave, and as they shuffle out the door of the café the oldest man stops to remark on our swimming.

'*Es war kalt, oder?*'

'*Nein,*' Anne and I reply in unison. We explain that it's summer to us, the water almost too warm. The man shakes his head, amused.

'*Badenixen!*' he calls to us as he walks off, laughing. I look to Anne in confusion. *Badenixen,* she explains, are bathing beauties, the pin-ups in swimsuits sprawled on the beach. I laugh, thinking of Esther Williams, of Bettie Page. Most of the year, I've swum in a clumsy, ill-fitting one-piece suit, my head capped in a woolly toque.

'We aren't *Badenixen,*' I reply.

But Anne goes on to tell me that *Nixe* means mermaid or siren, and I like this better. I think of the sirens and the water sprites: their song, their place amidst the flowers, amidst the rocks and the water. One interpretation of the German myth of Lorelei – whom Heinrich Heine's poem *Die Lorelei* depicted as a beautiful, distracting siren – speaks of a woman sitting by the water, drawing sailors to their deaths. The myths of sirens and mermaids take these sides: the woman in waiting, the temptress on the rocks.

A choice between an enclosed life of waiting and the wilderness is no choice at all. I think of the goddess Hertha, either bathing in her lake or drowning her suitors. I think of the sirens, who Ulysses so fiercely sought to evade.

Far better to be a siren than tied to the mast of a ship. Better to be at home in the water, the depth of the lake my wine-dark sea.

gift

Sixty kilometres south of Berlin, there is a landscape known as the Schenkenländchen. Stretching from Groß Köris in the north, Teupitz in the west, Briesen in the south, and Münchehofe in the east, the district is unified by its history: from 1330 until 1770, the land was acquired by and residence to the Schenk von Landsberg, one of Brandenburg's most powerful families. The name Schenkenländchen is derived from the family's name, *Schenk*, a title denoting nobility. *Ländchen* means 'little country' or 'little land', the diminutive *-chen* belying the vast moorlands of this stretch of Brandenburg.

Schenken traverses multiple meanings: from the Old High German *scanca*, for 'pipe', the word is linked to the pouring of wine, the funnelling of wine from a barrel. This connects to the family Schenk von Landsberg in as much as the title comes from *Mundschenk*, meaning 'cup-bearer'. The family was responsible for wine and beer provisions in the region. *Auschenk* means 'to pour out', and distantly, but not unrelatedly, *Geschenk*, which draws from the same root, means 'gift'. So I like to think that the Schenkenländchen is a generous gift of a landscape, wide and diverse, scattered with forests and sandy moorland, a wealth of lake water poured out over the Brandenburg sand.

Fontane arrived in the Schenkenländchen just before sunrise in 1862. The town – named for a Slavic word for either 'dull' or 'oak' – had been undersold to Fontane. Teupitz, he wrote, was beautiful – more so than the reports of an impoverished small town had led him to believe – and its lake was the source of the village's bounty. He found it simple, a sandy stretch scattered with pine and moss, the town of Teupitz slowly waking to the day. The region south of the village is a heathland.

I step off the train just south of there, in Halbe, the next stop down from Groß Köris. It is the first stop on a journey which will lead me to Teupitz, like Fontane. The station at Halbe is a concrete platform on a side street next to a factory. I don't expect much when I disembark, but as I wind my way through the town I find it quaint, with everything a small village might need. There is a travel agency, an insurance broker, a scattering of shops, and a bakery. I stop in and buy a *Quarkkrüstchen,* a small sweetened cake filled with quark cheese. It's a warm day, the sugar dissolves in my hands. I eat it greedily as I walk along Lindenstraße, my fingers coated in sweetness.

The town seems to have no central point of gravity. Every few hundred metres, a signpost details the history of refugees fleeing westward at the end of the Second World War. In the final days of the War, hundreds of thousands of Germans passed through Halbe. The confrontation between German and Soviet forces here – the Battle of Halbe – now goes mostly forgotten next to the Battle in Berlin.

Outside Halbe, the bodies of soldiers and civilians still lie unrecorded in the vast forests nearby, remnants of war just under the surface. Finding and laying them to rest is a continuing task. Halbe now has one of the largest German war-time cemeteries – some thirty thousand are buried here – and is growing due to efforts to identify remains found in mass graves or in the forest and to give them a proper burial. Staff from the Volksbund Deutsche Kriegsgräberfürsorge – the German War Graves Commission – work with metal detectors, diggers, and bomb disposal experts to scour the landscape. They find remains, soldiers' boots, dog tags. In one old East German history book I find in the Staatsbibliothek, it is said that after the battle, thousands of civilians – supported by the Soviets – were enrolled in giving the dead shallow burials in the forests. Now, some of the woods around Brandenburg hold the dead as if in waiting. I think about my paternal grandfather – 'Bampi', as the Welsh say – in France, exhausted by the war. I think of my maternal grandfather – 'Gung', as we say in Mandarin – flying fighter jets over China. In the intervening years they both moved countries, their children moved countries, and their grandchildren yet again. So much has changed in seven decades. But in Halbe I'm reminded that the landscape remembers, even as it grows over.

I follow the route of the 66-Seen-Wanderung towards Tornow in the west, just north of the cemetery. The pavement disappears and I find myself following the shoulder of a rural highway, the occasional gust of wind as a car blazes past. I check my map again, but it seems this is indeed the trail. A few kilometres west of here, it'll duck southwards into the trees. First, though, there's an overpass, the autobahn. I cross over it, the blazing sun casting its glare on the concrete, and then follow the shoulder of the road down on to a dirt track. I follow the trail markers south, past a house guarded by a Rottweiler and a Jack Russell terrier. And then I find the forest, quiet, alone. I move through the silence comfortably, carrying on in solitude as if it was something I'd always been able to do.

The pines are well spaced. Beneath them, a thick mat of reindeer lichen has spread, a grey carpet in the forest shade. The ground is dry – indeed, the lichen gives everything a dusty, matte finish – and the sunlight only appears in spare, thin shafts through the trees. I stick to the trail. I don't know this stretch of forest well.

The trail curves and leads me southward, tracing a kilometre in the trees. And then I find myself in an open field, the lamp-lined seam of a suburban road ahead of me. Tornow, a small village south-west of Halbe, appears as if out of nowhere, as if I'd walked through the forest to find this other world. The village streets turn to cobbles, each of which radiates from a central square. A community noticeboard and a bus shelter occupy prime position.

Tornower See sits at the end of one of these roads, a secluded and dark lake fringed by walking trails. A handful of private docks – *Betreten verboten* – line the edge of the lake. North of them, a small peninsula reaches into the water, a tiny, forested spit of land left open to the lake. I follow the trail down towards the shore, on my way passing a man at work with a shovel and a bag of mulch.

'*Ist es privat?*' I ask him. Is it private? I don't hear his reply clearly. What I hear is a muffled sentence, beginning with '*Nein,*' and ending with '*leider*'. I can't hear what's in between. I realise that he has either said, 'No, that would be unfortunate' or 'No, unfortunately it's not,' but I can't tell which. I nod awkwardly, unsure of what to say. I look at the man to determine whether he would rather I wasn't here, whether he thinks I'm an interloper at this town's quiet lake, but I can't tell. I wish him a good day and he wanders off.

At the bottom of the hill I find an enormous wooden dock, slanted and rusting into the lake. The water is dark, the kind of clear, refined blackness of deep lakes. I'm not sure what to expect. I don't know much about this one.

I undress and step out into the water, my feet disappearing beneath the soft sand. I draw my feet out and step farther into the deep, and then suddenly the ground drops off beneath me. I almost fall forwards but manage to brace myself, making a kind of clumsy dip into the water. The lake is cooler than Schermützelsee was last week, the darkness holding the cold, but I'm grateful for it. The day has been warm.

I bend my knees and swim out, not wanting to walk further and risk falling. It's free and clear as I swim out, but I can't see into its depths. My breath comes in heavy gasps. The water beneath me feels bottomless. I'm making panicked strokes. I am scared, I realise. It arrives unannounced. I haven't felt it in months. The tight grip of panic, when my mind sinks beneath the water's surface to whatever might be beneath. I lock my gaze above the water, trying to quiet my mind. The fear is real, but it isn't total.

I look to the shore and see no one. Tornow is quiet. Regaining control, I slip over on to my back, kicking my way towards the shore, fixating on the sky. The terror goes. I let the lake slip over my skin, and then I clamber back on to dry land. My skin tightens as I hit the air, goosebumps rolling over me. I watch the horizon, catching my breath.

Dressed again, I decide not to linger. I'll come back to this spot in summer – it is an incredibly secluded patch of shore-line – but for now, I want to walk. The swing of my own gait is a comfort. I want to move through the landscape, towards Teupitz, towards its lake. Fontane did it by coach, but I'll do it by foot.

The road out of Tornow takes me past a cluster of silent houses. Next to one, I find a book exchange box, a little wooden library at the side of the village road, marked with the words *Zum Mitnehmen.* 'To take.' I open it and find it full of books – most published in the GDR, price-marked for the East – their pages yellowing in the dry warmth. There's a Kipling, some Pushkin, and a more recent book of Georgia O'Keefe paintings. I wonder how long they've been here, if they've been in this village for decades. Brandenburg has a way of standing still. I close the lid gently, happily, the simple presence of these books a kind of comfort on my walk.

The road leads to another strip of houses, simple bunga-lows with ageing carports. In one, an old Trabi is painted in rainbow colours, its white body a base for a kaleido-scopic blaze of paint. It's a cheerful remnant, a relic not of mourning but of simple joy. I wonder when they got it – some people waited years. Perhaps they're just collectors, *Ostalgists*. I smile – the books, the car, small pleasures – and walk onwards towards Teupitz.

My walk through the Schenkenländchen is punctuated by information points. When I reach the end of the forest trail between Tornow and Teupitz, a noticeboard details 'Fontane's Teupitz', the short pages of the *Rambles* that have drawn so many to this lake-side town. Signposts mark out the routes of 'Fontane Walks' – indeed, there had been those in Buckow too – as though he were the patron saint of Brandenburg, breathing life into forgotten places. A nineteenth-century history, I realise, is refresh-ing, a kind of 'time before'. Across the road from one of the noticeboards, I find a small lane leading to the shore of Teupitzer See, the lake that Fontane described as the source of the village's fortunes.

When Fontane arrived in Teupitz, the lake was the cen-tral focus of his explorations. Without water, the village wouldn't have thrived as it did, with barges journeying up to Berlin carrying fruits, vegetables, peat and wood. The lake was so rich in fish and eels that in winter fishermen pulled nets beneath the ice, 'a feast for Teupitz'. But still the village retained a reputation as an 'ideal of poverty', a village untouched by the changing city nearby. After Fontane, of course, tourists came in droves.

I follow the lane along the eastern edge of the lake, past rows of gated gardens leading down to the water. Reeds form a seam on the horizon, the lake fringed with lashes of golden grass. The iron gates are all padlocked, the shore-line off limits. I recall Fontane's descriptions of boating here, from the tree-lined shallows to islands. It is different now, starker, the shore bursting with private docks. Farther down the lane, a small jetty reaches out into the lake – the water brown and clear – and I stop there, checking my map. Surely there is a place to swim. The jetty is concrete and lined with algae. There is no one around, I could manage a quick swim, but I'm sure this isn't the right place.

I back-track towards the information points. One of them had been a map. Tracing my fingers down the flattened image of the shore-line, I find the two parallel waved lines that denote a *Badestelle*, a 'swimming place'. It's farther down than I'd thought, a few hundred yards beyond the jetty. I retrace my route.

A tree-lined patch of lawn reaches down towards the beach. It is covered with geese. The lawn is scattered with their green shit. I walk towards the shore and the birds saunter off, waddling awkwardly towards the lake. They reach the water and paddle away, gathering fifty yards out as if waiting for me to leave, gossiping at a distance. I hear their calls slink back over the surface.

There's a bench at the edge of the water. I drop my bag on it and undress, piling my clothes neatly atop my bag, careful to avoid the goose shit. The lawn near my feet is littered with feathers. The birds aren't yet willing to cede territory to the summer swimmers.

I step into the cold, sandy shallows. It smells fishy, a bit of stagnant marsh, but I wade out farther until the water feels cleaner, less slick. I swim out, bumping my knees along the muddy bottom. It's shallow. A broad, flat kettle. Teupitzer See came from glaciers, but there are other kinds of lake nearby: lignite mines, clay pits, sand and gravel quarries. As monotonous as Brandenburg can be, its waters tell a scattered history.

I swim on my back for a while, watching the clouds work their way across the flat disc of the sun. I lie still in the shallow plate of Teupitzer See. With sadness and gratitude, an uneasy mixture, like oil and water, the thought arrives that I've only one lake left.

afterglow

When Germany was reunified in 1990, I was just four years old. I had never been to Germany and didn't know a word of German. Within a few years, however, through my sister's exchange trip to Germany, the country entered my life. A handful of years later, I made a similar trip to the Black Forest. At the time, I didn't learn to speak German much more than to say '*danke*' or '*tschüß*', thank you and goodbye. At the time, I had no sense of the world that had changed to the east. Even in living here now, when the seams are still visible – in the landscape, in the people, in the endless networks of bureaucracy – I can never truly understand what reunification has meant or continues to mean to the people of Berlin, Brandenburg and Germany more widely.

Weeks on from finishing my doctorate on Hampstead Heath, I've turned my attention to the landscape of Brandenburg. I've been reading reports from local regional planners, scientists and cultural historians. I leaf through blank-faced local publications at the Staatsbibliothek. My browser windows have been filled and slowed by PDFs about rural governance, lake restoration and cultural identity. I translate and read them all in scraps, paragraph by paragraph, cross-checking my translations with a dictionary, with Google Translate. I'm learning to work at the edge of my own words, where every sentence is a precarious and hard-fought gift. I'm learning to join one word to another, to situate meaning in unified territory.

In one of the reports, I read about the ways in which reunification transformed local governance. In 1952, East German administrative districts were drastically – and arbitrarily – redrawn. *Bezirke* – districts – included both urban and rural communities, often overwriting communities linked by unified history, culture or landscape. After reunification, borders were again redrawn, local governance and administration transformed once more. In the landscape, this has meant new forms of connection: regions united by tourist boards, by environmental preservation, by regional parks.

North of Berlin, in the stretch of Brandenburg scattered with turquoise green lakes, one such district has come into existence. Barnim – a district created from the former GDR districts of Bernau and Eberswalde – stretches across the north of Berlin, as far east as the Polish border. It rests atop the Barnim Plateau of clay and sand, across moraines formed by glaciation. So Barnim, before being an administrative district, was a place in the landscape. But during the GDR, Barnim did not exist on paper. In the ground, perhaps, and in historical identity, but as a collective identity and a collective memory, Barnim disappeared. Its re-emergence now – in local government, in the co-ordinated parks and landscape strategies that characterise this stretch of forests and lakes – is one of the ways in which identity has been reforged, one of the ways in which unification efforts have been laid over the land. Names – those reclaimed, those erased – are one of the ways in which *die Wende*, 'the turn' from two Germanys into one, shaped not just a people but also a landscape.

Hellsee is a lake in Barnim. Ten kilometres north of Bernau, in a wide swathe of mixed forest, it sits winding, crooked and sloped amidst the trees. Like Liepnitzsee, to its west, it forms part of a glacial chain, a series of crenulated lakes formed in the Weichselian glaciation. Long and skinny, it is a lake that catches the light, unfurling as it does amidst the beech-wood and alders. It has a name that captures it: 'Bright Lake'.

I wake up to the sound of a bumble bee. The cherry laurel shrubs in the courtyard have begun to bloom: conical, snow-coloured inflorescences speckling the dark-green leaves. The bees haven't left for days. With my window open a crack, the sound of them rushes in. From my bed, the city is silent but for the bees.

The gauze of the curtains does little; the room is filled with light. When I close my eyes, it remains bright, a sure sign of a sunny day. I linger a minute, watching the morning, and then throw off the duvet. It is bright. Appropriate, I think.

The mornings of lake days have become routine: coffee, half poured into a cup and half poured into a thermos. Toast. I nibble at it haphazardly as I pack lunch. Bread, cheese, eggs. I've got chocolate today, so I pack that too. My bag fills: lunch, towel, a plastic bag. I've learned something about preparation over the year and also pack a change of clothes.

I slide my bag on to the rack of my green bicycle and slip out, locking the door behind me. It's a thirty-kilometre journey, leading first through the northern stretch of Prenzlauer Berg and then on through Weißensee. I follow the bike lane past the turn-off for Weißer See, a smile growing into the corners of my mouth. Anne and I have taken to swimming there on weekdays, like I used to do with Jacob. A convivial intimacy has grown into the place that had held sadness. Joy too. Last week, as we swam from the shore towards the raft that houses the fountain, the enormous jut of white water came to life, springing fifty feet into the air in front of us. It scared the wits out of Anne and me, and we floated laughing wholeheartedly at the surface of the lake.

I pass the turn-off and slip further north, ducking between the skinny tram tracks that lead out towards Karow. Here, the bike lane joins the pavement, and I cycle along dodging weekend walkers and the overgrowing hedges that lean out over it. May is brimming over. The houses of the city give way to fields of golden rape. The chestnuts are dappled with spikes of pink flower. The air is a musk of lilac. The cherries have already finished, their pale remains carpeting the ground. I count the young leaves of linden as I pass them, my favourite tree spreading itself across the city. As I pass each plant, I name it: *Raps. Kastanien. Flieder. Kirsche. Linde.*

At Karow, I stop to check my map. In the year of

swimming, I have not rectified the problem of travelling without a paper one: I pull out my phone, reluctantly sliding my fingers over the webbing of roads that covers the city. I feel no shame about it any more. I have a small book of lakes and trails in my bag that I rarely look at. The frail enormity of a paper map wouldn't serve me well on my bike, and I can never fold them properly anyway. Instead, I'm a small blue dot, pulsing and bright like the lakes.

The route through Buch leads me down a road so poorly cobbled I have to walk. The stones slip in and out of their places. Pools of pitch have been laid over the gaps. It is a road that feels as though it has been at a standstill, like the sand tracks of Brandenburg, the places untransformed. At the end of the road, there is a forest track, and beyond that, a country road lined with fields.

I'm singing: repeating the first verse of 'Land Of The Silver Birch' to myself as I pedal. My foot hits the bottom of its rotation with every *Boomdiddy-ah-da*. As it is my last new lake – for now, at least – I wonder if I ought to sing a song about Berlin and Brandenburg, so I rewrite the song as I cycle, singing the verses in alternation, lingering with pleasure over my silly lines:

Land of the pine and birch,
Home of the bear
Where now the mighty wolf wanders again
Blue lake and sandy shore
I will return once more
Boomdiddy-ah-da, Boomdiddy-ah-da,
Boomdiddy-ah-da, eh.

Within an hour, my voice exhausted, I reach Bernau. Its *Plattenbau* houses rise in the periphery of my vision. I pass the curving arc of the old town fortress and turn northwards, following Ladeburger Chaussee out of the town, towards a field of wind turbines. I've never been here without rain.

It is hot today, and a dry wind is cutting across the fields, dredging up the dust. It rolls sidelong across the flats on either side of the road, near the Lobetal bunker. I hold my breath as I cycle through it, the thick cloud of red dust swirling over me. On the other side of the fields, the air is clear.

At Lobetal, near Mechesee, I cut into the woods. I can hear the bells from the forest church ringing, rhythmic and distant as a bird call. It echoes through the pines. The road turns to track, lined with dried pine needles and caked with mounds of soft white sand. I ride my bike for a few hundred yards and then slow, hopping off to a walk. The trail towards Hellsee is thick and pillowed. I'll take my time with it.

The pines thicken towards Mechesee, and as the trail dips towards the top of the lake – near where I swam some weeks ago, when it was still cold – I follow the trail markers for the 66-Seen-Wanderung. Three other trail markers are painted on to the trees – red stripes, green stripes, the blue circle of the 66-Seen and one in yellow – so I keep an eye out, careful to take the trail that runs northward. The track is joined by a smaller trail, where a man on a bicycle with battered panniers wheels past me, speeding ahead. A few moments later, he appears again, back-tracking and lost.

'*Wohin fährst du?*' I ask him. Where are you riding to? He looks at me in confusion.

'*Wo ist der Weg?*' he asks me. Where is the trail? I ask him which trail he wants, as there are a few, and point in the direction of each of them. Hearing my accent, he looks at me in confusion, as if he doesn't quite believe me. I see his brow furrow, and then he shakes his head and wanders off. I wonder if perhaps he doesn't trust me, a foreigner in his home landscape. I think of Fontane, lamenting the idea that someone from abroad might write his home landscape first. But I know the trail here.

I carry on, past a plantation of larches that appear beaded and decorated in the sunlight, and on past a marshy stretch of brook scattered with alder. It isn't as dramatic as the alder carr along the Briese, but it has the same winding, otherworldly quality. The trees create dark and dappled shadows on the water's surface. Everything else is green.

The trail veers westward and turns into a narrow paved lane. Fishing huts appear on one side – some cared for, some neglected – and then, at the end of the narrow track I can see it: Hellsee, Bright Lake, aglow in sunlight. It needs a brighter word than bright.

In Margaret Atwood's *Surfacing*, the young protagonist – she never gets a name – goes back to her home island on a remote Canadian lake, searching for her father. She doesn't find what she came for. I've been reading and re-reading this book all year, as if it might hold a key. I've carried a paperback of it, battered and dog-eared, in my bag. I've carried it in lieu of a map.

She grows ever wilder, retreating from her friends, retreating from her lover, rushing into the wilderness. She strips off her clothes, throws away her shoes and runs into the forest. She swims in the lake and sees its horrors and joys: it emboldens her to cast off the trappings of the good life she is pretending she can live. Home is gone, but so too is the possibility of pretending that pain hasn't changed her.

I've been troubled by these narratives of women walking out on their lives, exiling themselves in order to take up space. I'm worried by the idea that in order to find a place for themselves, women walk away, as if the only choice is between the room of one's own or the inexorable, unequivocal wild. Between Penelope and the sirens. But likewise I've lingered over Atwood's lines, wondering whether my decision to swim was a way of surfacing from a suffocating pain, a way of marking territory. The ghosts can't be exorcised, though, and there isn't any wilderness left to claim. Though pain alleviates with time, fear remains, rolling as if on the tide.

I never left my life. At the end of each journey, I went back to work, back to my friends, back to my home in Berlin. That the lakes could exist alongside all of this made them more valuable to me. They became points of light in the landscape, generous, steady and incalculably beautiful.

At the edge of Hellsee, the shallows are clear. A school of young perch are darting between the reeds, the flash of their red tails catching the light. I want to be like them, swift in the water.

I wander the edge of the lake until I find a fallen pine, enormous and stripped of its bark. It reaches out into the lake, bleached white in the sun, smoothed by the winter. This small curve in the shore is lined by beeches. On one side, a single alder tree reaches out over the water. This is the spot.

I lay my clothes by the roots of the pine, piled as usual atop my bag. Glancing along the trail in either direction, I see that I am alone. It is still early in the season. I slip towards the lake's edge, stepping knee-deep into the water. Warmth surrounds me, and then the slightest wisp of cold.

I swim out, pressing my hands through the turquoise clarity of the lake, moving towards its centre. From here, I can see the line of Hellsee as it curves and narrows on either end. The water rounds a corner and disappears behind the forest.

I linger here, afloat and watching the trees. Feeling the depth of the lake beneath me, I slip on to my back. I watch the sky, sensing the cool of the water as I move through it. Suspended, I drift home.

bibliography

The following texts proved invaluable in the process of writing this book:

Atwood, Margaret, *Surfacing*, Virago Press, London (2009 edition. First published 1979). Extract reproduced by kind permission of Margaret Atwood.

Berdahl, Daphne, *Where the World Ended: Re-Unification and Identity in the German Borderland*, University of California Press, Berkeley (1999)

Bernhardt, Juliane; Engelhardt, Christof; Kirillin, Georgiy; Matschullat, Jörg, 'Lake Ice Phenology in Berlin-Brandenburg from 1947–2007: Observations and Model Hindcasts', pp791–817, *Climactic Change* 112 (2012)

Blackbourn, David, *The Conquest of Nature: Water, Landscape and the Making of Modern Germany*, Jonathan Cape, London (2006)

Blankennagel, Jens, '66-Seen-Wanderweg in Brandenburg: Einmal rund um Berlin', *Berliner Zeitung* (17 October 2014)

Boehrer, Bertram, and Schultze, Martin, 'Stratification of Lakes', pp1–27, *Reviews of Geophysics* 46, no. 2 (2008)

Brockmann, Jan, 'Sand. Water. Wind', pp5–22, *Raw: Architectural Engagements with Nature*, edited by Solveig Bøe, Hege Charlotte Faber and Brit Strandhagen, Routledge, London (2016)

Coates, Peter, 'Borderland: No-Man's Land, Nature's Wonderland: Troubled Humanity and Untroubled Earth', pp499–516, *Environment and History* 20, no. 4 (2014)

Conrad, Andreas, 'Heiligabend wurde die Grenze geöffnet', *Der Taggespiegel* (23 December 2014)

Cruikshank, Julie, *Do Glaciers Listen?: Local Knowledge, Colonial Encounters, and Social Imagination*, University of British Columbia Press, Vancouver (2005)

Darby, David, 'Theodor Fontane und die Vernetzung der Welt die Mark Brandenburg zwischen Vormoderne und Moderne', pp145–164, *Metropole, Provinz und Welt: Raum und Mobilität in der Literatur des Realismus*, edited by Roland Berbig and Dirk Göttsche, Walter der Gruyter, Berlin (2013)

Deakin, Roger, *Waterlog: A Swimmer's Journey Through Britain*, Vintage, London (2000)

Detrich, H. William, ed., 'Antarctica: Life on Ice', Special Issue, *Scientific American Classics* 26 (2014)

Dortmann, Andrea, *Winter Facets: Traces and Tropes of the Cold*, Peter Lang AG, Bern (2007)

Driescher, Eva; Behrendt, Horst; Schellenberger, Günter, and Stellmacher, Rita, 'Lake Müggelsee and its Environment: Natural Conditions and Anthropogenic Impacts', pp327–343, *Internationale Revue der gesamten Hydrobiologie und Hydrographie* 78, no. 3 (1993)

Fontane, Theodor, *Effi Briest*, translated by Hugh Rorrison and Helen Chambers, Penguin, London (1995)

Fontane, Theodor, *The Stechlin*, translated by William L. Zwiebel, Camden House, Rochester (1995)

Fontane, Theodor, *Wanderungen durch die Mark Brandenburg*, 4 Volumes, Wilhelm Hertz, Berlin (1862–1882)

'Forum: The Nature of German Environmental History', pp113–130, *German History* 27, no. 1 (2009)

Gopnik, Adam, *Winter: Five Windows on the Season*, House of Anansi Press, Toronto (2011)

Hutchinson, G. Evelyn, *A Treatise on Limnology*, 3 Volumes, John Wiley and Sons, New York (1957)

Kirbach, Roland, 'Die Seeschlacht', *Die Zeit* (1 June 2011)

Kögel, Annette, 'Der erste Sommer der Freiheit', *Der Taggespiegel* (23 August 2015)

Krümmelbein, Julia; Bens, Oliver; Raab, Thomas, and Naeth, M. Anne, 'A History of Lignite Mining and Reclamation Practices in Lusatia, Eastern Germany', pp53-66, *Canadian Journal of Soil Science* 92 (2012)

Landesamt für Bergbau, Geologie und Rohstoffe Brandenburg, *Brandenburgische Geowissenschaftliche Beiträge 2: Ein Streifzug durch die Historie des Braunkohlentiefbaus in Ostbrandenburg*, LBGR Brandenburg, Cottbus (2012)

Lekan, Thomas M., 'Imagining the Nation in Nature: Landscape Preservation and German Identity, 1890-1945', PhD Dissertation, University of Wisconsin-Madison (1999)

Lekan, Thomas, and Zeller, Thomas, 'Region, Scenery, and Power: Cultural Landscapes in Environmental History', pp332–365, *The Oxford Handbook of Environmental History*, edited by Andrew C. Isenberg, Oxford University Press, Oxford (2014)

Mietz, Olaf, *Allgemeiner hydrogeographisch-limnologischer Überblick über die Seen Brandenburgs und die Entwicklung eines Klassifikationsmodells für die glazialen Seen des Norddeutschen Tieflandes*,

Institüt für angewandte Gewässerökologie in Brandenburg, Potsdam (1996)

Nelson, Arvid, *Cold War Ecology: Forests, Farms, and People in the East German Landscape, 1945–1989*, Yale University Press, New Haven (2005)

Nixdorf, Brigitte; Hemm, Mike; Hoffmann, Anja, and Richter, Peggy, *Dokumentation von Zustand und Entwicklung der wichtigsten Seen Deutschlands*, Umweltbundesamt, Dessau-Roßlau (2004)

Nixdorf, Brigitte; Hemm, Mike; Schlundt, Anja; Kapfer, Maria, and Krumbeck, Hartwig, *Braunkohlentagebauseen in Deutschland*, Brandenburgische Technische Universität Cottbus, Cottbus (2000)

O'Sullivan, P. E., and Reynolds, C. S. eds, *The Lakes Handbook: Limnology and Limnetic Ecology*, Blackwell, Oxford (2004)

Pfannkuche, Jens; Meisel, Jen, and Mietz, Olaf, 'Factors Affecting Clarity of Freshwater Lakes in Brandenburg, Germany', pp311–321, *Limnologica* 30 (2000)

Reschke, Manfred, *66-Seen-Wanderung*, Trescher Verlag, Berlin (2014)

Rilke, Rainer Maria, 'The Gazelle' translation copyright © 1982 by Stephen Mitchell; from *Selected Poetry of Rainer Maria Rilke*, translated by Stephen Mitchell. Used by permission of Random House, an imprint and division of Penguin Random House LLC. All rights reserved. Any third party use of this material, outside of this publication, is prohibited. Interested parties must apply directly to Penguin Random House LLC for permission.

Röhring, Andreas, 'Cultural landscape as action arena – an identity-based concept of region-building', a paper presented at the Regional Studies Association Annual Conference, Newcastle, United Kingdom (April 2011) bibliography

Schaer, Cathrin, 'Landscaping the Death Strip: A Vision of the Berlin Wall as a Giant Garden', *Spiegel Online* (2 July 2009)

Scheer, Regina, *Der Umgang mit den Denkmälern: Eine Recherche in Brandenburg*, Brandenburgische Landeszentrale für politische Bildung und Ministerium für Wissenschaft, Forschung und Kultur, Potsdam (2003)

Schiemeier, Quirin, 'Life Discovered Under Ice in Antarctic Lake', *Nature* (12 February 2013) http://www.scientificamerican.com/article/life-discovered-under-ice-in-antarctic-lake/

Senate Department for Urban Development and the Environment, *Geological Outline*, Senate Department for Urban Development and the Environment, Berlin (2013)

Stefansson, Vilhjalmur, 'Encyclopedia Arctica', 15-volume unpublished reference work, Dartmouth: Dartmouth College Library, http://collections.dartmouth.edu/arctica-beta/index.html

Sussmann, Hans, *Teupitz und das Schenkenländchen*, Stadt Teupitz, Teupitz (1973)

Stiftung Berliner Mauer, 'Denkmallandschaft Berliner Mauer', Berlin (2013) http://denkmallandschaft-berliner-mauer.de

Talling, J. F., 'The Developmental History of Inland-Water Science', pp119–141, *Freshwater Reviews* 1 (2008)

Terry, Andrew; Ullrich, Karin, and Riecken, Uwe, *The Green Belt of Europe: From Vision to Reality*, IUCN, Cambridge (2006)

Tsing, Anna, *The Mushroom at the End of the World: On The Possibility of Life in Capitalist Ruins,* Princeton University Press, Princeton (2015)

Tyb'l, Lothar, *Teupitz am See: ein Schatz in der Mark Brandenburg*, Weissensee Verlag, Berlin (2006)

Tyler, John E., 'The Secchi Disc', pp1–6, *Limnology and Oceanography* 13, no. 1 (1968)

Wallis, Emma, 'Digging Up The Past in Halbe', *Deutsche Welle* (24 April 2013)

Wall Kimmerer, Robin, *Gathering Moss: A Natural and Cultural History of Mosses*, Oregon State University Press, Corvallis (2003)

Walther, Peter, ed., *Märkische Dichterlandschaft: Ein illustrierter Literaturführer durch die Mark Brandenburg*, Deutsche Verlags-Anstalt, Stuttgart (1998)

Wiechers, Katharina, 'Der unendliche Uferstreit vom Groß Glienicker See', *Der Taggespiegel* (3 July 2014)

Wordsworth, William, *A Guide to the Lakes*, 5th Edition, Henry Frowde, London (1906)

acknowledgements

A great number of people made this book possible. To my editor, Lennie Goodings: thank you for your guidance, insight and passion for this book. Thanks also to Nicole Winstanley and Kathrin Liedtke for your enthusiasm and encouragement. To my agent, David Godwin, thank you for taking a chance on me.

I'm grateful to those who helped make this process a pleasure and advised me along the way. Lisette Verhagen and Philippa Sitters at DGA, Tamsyn Berryman at Virago, everyone at Godshot in Immanuelkirchstraße, Michael Monaghan, David Darby, Belinda Bowring, Kelsey Padjen, Simon Connolly, Amy Raphael, Joanna Sidhu, Ruby Stocklin-Weinberg, Darren Patrick, Justin Kinnear, Stefan Fergus, Luca Bendandi, Sennah Yee, Joy Xiang, Steffi Ackermann, Katrin Hahner, Ricardo Rivas, Joan Steiger-wald, Cate Sandilands, Beth Moore – thank you. Thanks especially to friends who read and commented on drafts of the manuscript: Alyssa Mackenzie, Rachel Hopwood,

Cassandra Hogan, David Balzer and Anne Haeming. You made this a better book. You all helped me stay afloat.

This book began as an experiment, for me, in non-academic writing. Thanks to Paul Sullivan for wholeheartedly embracing my proposal to blog about the lakes for *Slow Travel Berlin*. Thanks to everyone who followed the 52 Lakes Project on social media – your kind words propelled me. *Sehr vielen Dank* to all the Berliners and Brandenburgers who recommended lakes and offered guidance on local history. I'm so grateful to live here and for all the kindness I've received along the way. Any errors in my account of this place and its past are entirely my own.

To my family, I couldn't have done any of this without your support and patience. Mom, Dad, Nika, Pauline, Daniel, Amanda, Dilan, James: I'm so proud to be a part of this family, even though we're all far apart. Thank you for everything you've given me. *Wǒ ài nǐ.* I love you so much.